MASSACHUSETTS TEST PREP
Narrative Writing Workbook
A Complete Guide to Writing Stories, Personal Narratives, and More
Grade 4

© 2017 by Test Master Press Massachusetts

All rights reserved. No part of this book may be reproduced or transmitted in any form or by any means, electronic, mechanical, photocopying, recording, or otherwise without prior written permission.

ISBN 978-1979745901

CONTENTS

Introduction	**4**
Developing Writing Skills	**5**
Warm-Up Exercise: Relating Events to Each Other	6
Set 1: Understanding Plot	7
Warm-Up Exercise: Problems and Solutions	12
Set 2: Using a Main Problem	13
Warm-Up Exercise: Using the Setting	18
Set 3: Understanding Setting	19
Warm-Up Exercise: Characters Traits and Problems	24
Set 4: Creating a Main Character	25
Warm-Up Exercise: Using Details to Show Feelings	30
Set 5: Using Descriptions	32
Set 6: Using Dialogue	38
Warm-Up Exercise: Characters Learning Lessons	44
Set 7: Understanding Theme	45
Set 8: Starting Strong	50
Warm-Up Exercise: Choosing Descriptive Words	58
Warm-Up Exercise: Choosing Action Words	59
Set 9: Using Concrete Details	60
Set 10: Using Sensory Details	66
Set 11: Using a Narrator	72
Warm-Up Exercise: Using Transition Words	78
Set 12: Understanding Sequence	79
Applying Writing Skills	**84**
Set 13: Write from a Picture Prompt	86
Set 14: Write a Personal Narrative	94
Set 15: Write an Animal Story	102
Set 16: Write an Adventure Story	106
Set 17: Write a Diary Entry	110
Set 18: Write a Fantasy Story	114
Set 19: Write a Science Fiction Story	118
Set 20: Write a Mystery Story	122
Set 21: Write a Real-Life Story	126
Set 22: Write a Letter	130
Writing Review and Scoring Guide	**134**

INTRODUCTION
For Parents, Teachers, and Tutors

About the Book

This workbook will develop strong narrative writing skills and give students the ability to produce effective narratives of all types. The first section will develop the essential narrative writing skills one by one. The second section allows students to apply these skills and gives students practice creating writing of several styles and in many genres.

By completing the writing tasks in this book, students will be able to create writing that meets the requirements listed in the state standards and respond effectively to all types of writing prompts.

State Standards for Writing

The 2017 *Massachusetts Curriculum Frameworks* divide writing skills based on text type and purpose. The three types of writing are opinion pieces, informative/explanatory texts, and narrative writing. This book focuses on narrative writing, and has been specifically created based on the skills listed in the standards. The exercises and tasks will develop all the skills described in the standards and ensure that students are able to produce writing with the key characteristics expected.

Developing Writing Skills

The first section of the book contains twelve sets of five writing prompts. Each set is focused on one key element of narrative writing. The first task in each set introduces the skill and guides students through the task. Students then master the skill by completing the four additional writing tasks. Many of the sets also include a warm-up exercise to prepare students for the set, to introduce and develop a key skill, or to help students focus on a key characteristic of narrative writing.

Applying Writing Skills

The second section of the book contains ten sets of four writing prompts. Each set is focused on one style or one genre of narrative writing. Students will use the key elements of narrative writing and apply the skills they have learned. Hints and tips are also included throughout the section to guide students. As well as developing general writing skills, this section will prepare students for the types of writing tasks found on assessment tasks and tests.

Preparing for the MCAS English Language Arts Test

Students will be assessed each year by taking a set of tests known as the MCAS English Language Arts assessments. The MCAS tests include writing tasks where students write narratives. This workbook will ensure that students have the skills and experience to produce narrative compositions with the features expected of student writing.

Developing Writing Skills

The exercises in this section will develop the writing skills needed to produce all types of narrative writing. Each set focuses on developing one specific skill.

Follow the instructions for each writing prompt. In some cases, you will write your work in the space provided. In other cases, you will write your work on a separate sheet of paper, or type your work.

Warm-Up Exercise: Relating Events to Each Other

In the first set, you will learn about the plots of stories. A story's plot is the set of events that occur. These events occur in order and are related to each other. They fit together to form a complete story. Each diagram below shows the three events of a story. Finish each plot by completing the empty box with an event that makes sense.

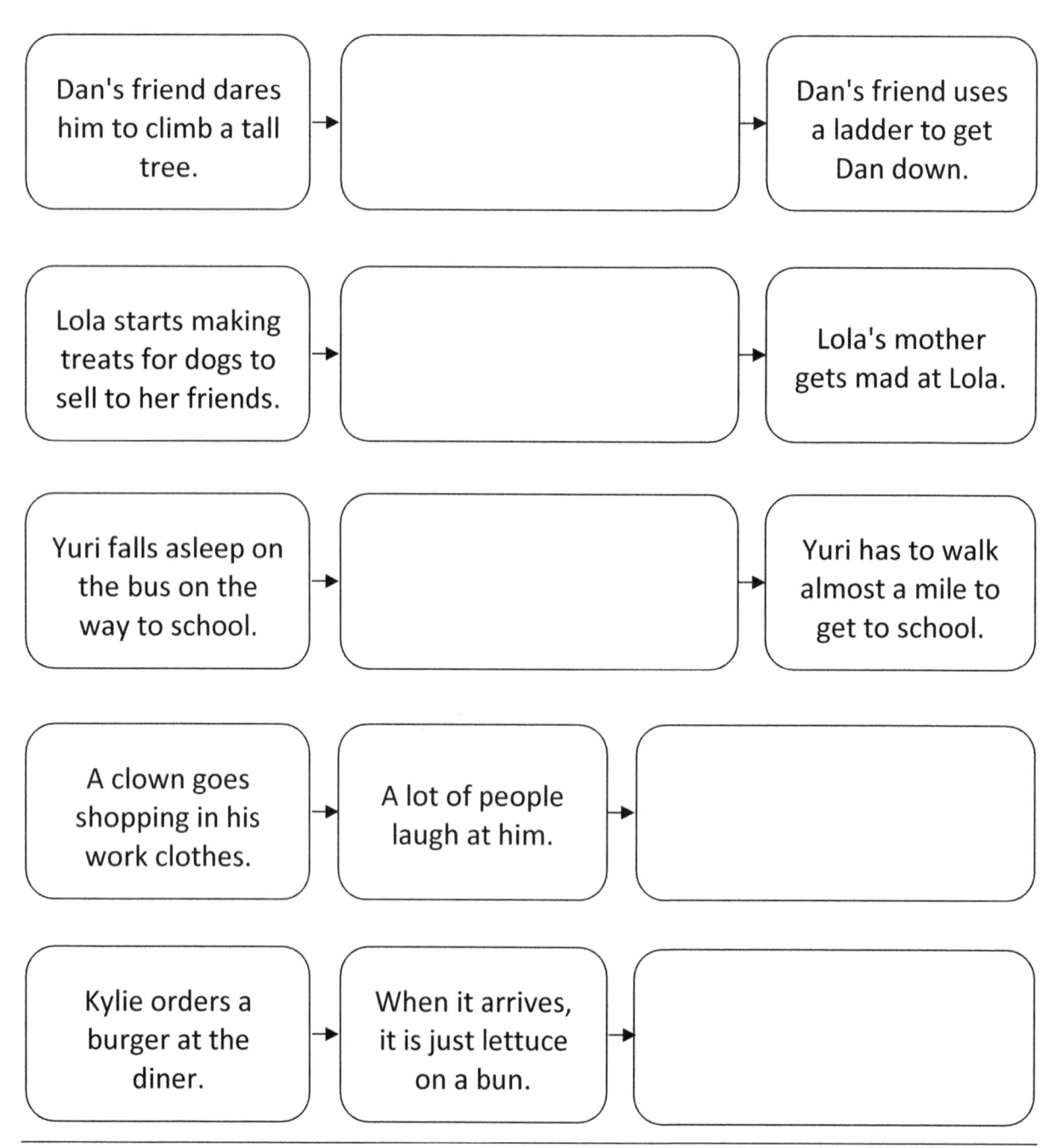

| Dan's friend dares him to climb a tall tree. | → | | → | Dan's friend uses a ladder to get Dan down. |

| Lola starts making treats for dogs to sell to her friends. | → | | → | Lola's mother gets mad at Lola. |

| Yuri falls asleep on the bus on the way to school. | → | | → | Yuri has to walk almost a mile to get to school. |

| A clown goes shopping in his work clothes. | → | A lot of people laugh at him. | → | |

| Kylie orders a burger at the diner. | → | When it arrives, it is just lettuce on a bun. | → | |

Set 1: Understanding Plot

Writing Prompt 1

The plot of a story is what happens in a story. It is the sequence of events that occur in the story. Read the plot below.

Carla wins a contest. She goes to her favorite band's concert.

The sentences above describe the main events that occur in the story in order. First, Carla wins the contest. Then Carla goes to the concert.

The table below shows a story a student planned with this plot. The plan gives more details about what happened.

Use the plan below to write a story. Write or type a story of about 1 page.

The Beginning: Describe what happens first.
Carla receives a phone call. She learns that she has won a contest. She gets to see the band Great Scott perform.
→ **Start your story by writing a paragraph that describes these events.**
The Middle: Describe what happens next.
Carla goes to the concert. She has a great time. She gets to meet the band as well.
→ **Write two or three paragraphs that describe these events.**
The Ending: Describe what happens in the end.
Carla is tired after a long day. She goes to sleep thinking it was one of the best days ever.
→ **End your story by writing a paragraph that describes these events.**

Writing Prompt 2

Write a story with the plot described below.

Jenny collects coins. She finds a rare coin at a yard sale for a cheap price.

Start by thinking about the details of your story. Think about what Jenny does once she finds the coin. Think about how she feels about the find.

Use the table below to plan your story. Write or type a story of about 1 page.

The Beginning: Describe how Jenny finds the coin.
→ **Start your story by writing a paragraph that describes these events.**
The Middle: Describe what Jenny does when she finds the coin.
→ **Write two or three paragraphs that describe these events.**
The Ending: Describe how Jenny feels at the end.
→**End your story by writing a paragraph that shows how Jenny feels.**

Writing Prompt 3

Write a story with the plot described below.

Terry tries to make a clay vase, but things go wrong.

Use the table below to plan your story. Write or type a story of about 1 page.

The Beginning: Describe how Terry is making a clay vase.   → **Start your story by writing a paragraph that introduces what is happening.**
The Middle: Describe what goes wrong with the clay vase.   → **Write two or three paragraphs that describe these events.**
The Ending: Describe what Terry does in the end.   →**End your story by writing a paragraph that describes these events.**

Writing Prompt 4

Write a story with the plot described below.

Chris's sister Jane is afraid of storms. He tries to calm her during a large storm.

Use the table below to plan your story. Write or type a story of about 1 page.

The Beginning: Describe the storm and how Jane is afraid.   → **Start your story by writing a paragraph that introduces what is happening.**
The Middle: Describe how Chris tries to calm Jane.   → **Write two or three paragraphs that describe these events.**
The Ending: Describe what happens in the end.   →**End your story by writing a paragraph that describes these events.**

Writing Prompt 5

Write a story with the plot described below.

Mario is swimming at the beach. He goes out too far and has to be rescued.

Use the table below to plan your story. Write or type a story of about 1 page.

The Beginning: Describe how Mario is swimming at the beach.
→ Start your story by writing a paragraph that introduces what is happening.
The Middle: Describe how Mario goes out too far and need to be rescued.
→ Write two or three paragraphs that describe these events.
The Ending: Describe how Mario is rescued in the end.
→End your story by writing a paragraph that describes these events.

Warm-Up Exercise: Problems and Solutions

In the next set, you will write stories that describe how a problem is solved. There are many ways that a problem could be solved. You can come up with good story ideas by writing a list of ways the problem could be solved. Then you can choose one from your list to use in your story. Practice coming up with story ideas by listing four ways that a character might solve each problem below.

1. Erica misses her sister Beth when Beth goes away to college.

   Erica could start writing letters to Beth every day.

   _____

   _____

   _____

2. Aaron keeps getting woken up by his neighbor's barking dog.

   _____

   _____

   _____

   _____

3. Clayton needs to cross a river, but there is no bridge.

   _____

   _____

   _____

   _____

Set 2: Using a Main Problem

Writing Prompt 6

Many stories are based around a main problem. The start of the story describes the main problem. The middle of the story describes how the character tries to solve the problem. The end of the story describes how the problem is solved. Read the problem below.

Amanda wants to work in class, but her friend Jordan talks all the time.

The sentence above describes the problem. There are many ways that Amanda could try to solve this problem. The table below shows a story a student planned based on this problem.

Use the plan below to write a story. Write or type a story of about 1 page.

The Beginning: Describe the main problem.
Amanda wants to do her work in class. Her friend Jordan sits next to her. Jordan talks to Amanda all the time.
→ **Start your story by writing a paragraph that introduces the problem.**
The Middle: Describe how Amanda tries to solve the problem.
Amanda asks another friend Ava to sit with them. Ava also talks a lot. Ava and Jordan now talk to each other all the time, while Amanda does her work.
→ **Write two or three paragraphs that describe these events.**
The Ending: Describe what happens in the end to solve the problem.
Amanda is pleased that her plan worked. Ava and Jordan are happy to always be talking.
→**End your story by writing a paragraph that shows that the problem is solved.**

Writing Prompt 7

Write a story based on the problem below.

Chan has to share a computer with his sister. He never gets enough time on it.

There are many ways that Chan could solve this problem. Start by thinking of different ways that Chan could solve the problem. Then choose the idea you want to base your story on.

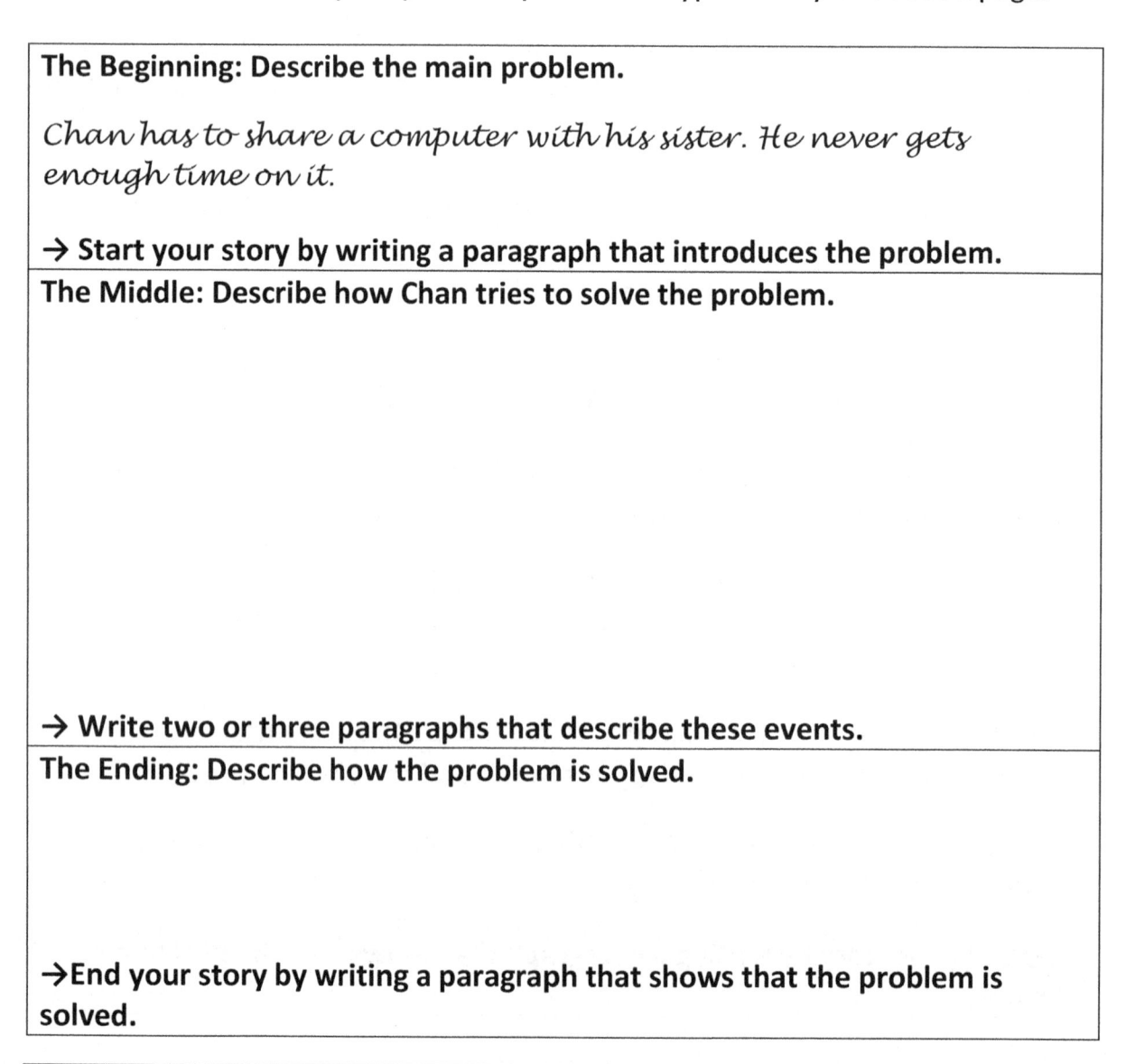

Use the table below to plan your story. Write or type a story of about 1 page.

The Beginning: Describe the main problem.   *Chan has to share a computer with his sister. He never gets enough time on it.*   → **Start your story by writing a paragraph that introduces the problem.**
The Middle: Describe how Chan tries to solve the problem.   → **Write two or three paragraphs that describe these events.**
The Ending: Describe how the problem is solved.   →**End your story by writing a paragraph that shows that the problem is solved.**

Writing Prompt 8

Imagine that someone has a very messy room. Think of a problem this might cause. Write a story about the problem and how it is solved.

Use the table below to plan your story. Write or type a story of about 1 page.

The Beginning: Describe the main problem.   → **Start your story by writing a paragraph that introduces the problem.**
The Middle: Describe how the character tries to solve the problem.   → **Write two or three paragraphs that describe these events.**
The Ending: Describe how the problem is solved.   →**End your story by writing a paragraph that shows that the problem is solved.**

Writing Prompt 9

Write a story based on the problem below.

> Jenna's mother seems to use every pot and pan when she cooks.
> Jenna is tired of having to wash everything up.

Use the table below to plan your story. Write or type a story of about 1 page.

The Beginning: Describe the main problem.   *Jenna's mother seems to use every pot and pan when she cooks. Jenna is tired of having to wash everything up.*   **→ Start your story by writing a paragraph that introduces the problem.**
The Middle: Describe how Jenna tries to solve the problem.   **→ Write two or three paragraphs that describe these events.**
The Ending: Describe how the problem is solved.   **→End your story by writing a paragraph that shows that the problem is solved.**

Writing Prompt 10

Write a story based on the problem below.

> Andy is having dinner at his friend's house. The food looks weird. He does not want to be rude, but he is scared of the food.

Use the table below to plan your story. Write or type a story of about 1 page.

The Beginning: Describe the main problem.   *Andy is having dinner at his friend's house. The food looks weird. He does not want to be rude, but he is scared of the food.*   → **Start your story by writing a paragraph that introduces the problem.**
The Middle: Describe how Andy tries to solve the problem.   → **Write two or three paragraphs that describe these events.**
The Ending: Describe how the problem is solved.   →**End your story by writing a paragraph that shows that the problem is solved.**

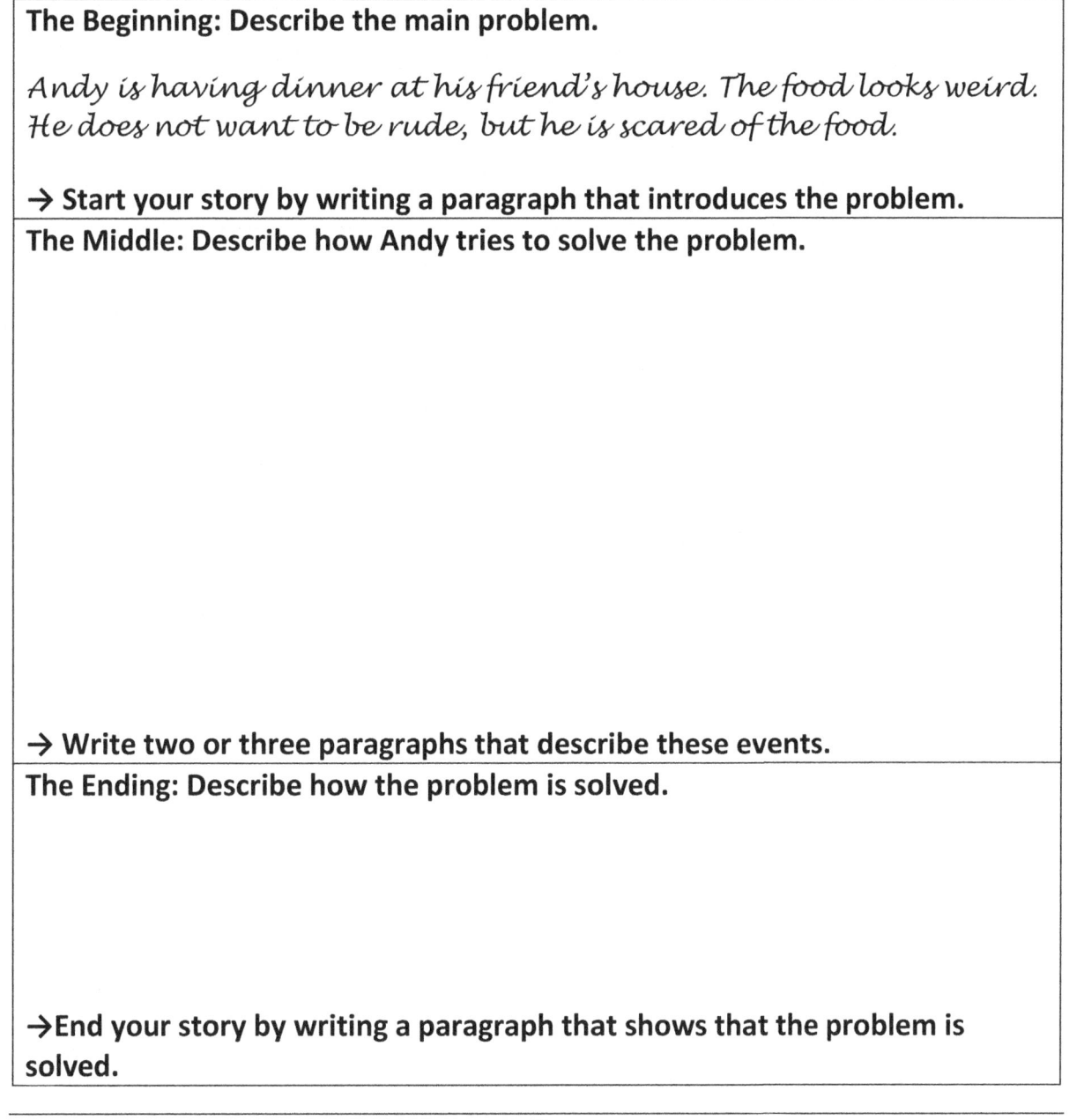

Narrative Writing Workbook, Grade 4

Warm-Up Exercise: Using the Setting

In the next set, you will learn about setting. Remember that the setting is not what the story is about, but just where and when the events happen. When you need to come up with a story idea from a setting, think about something interesting that might happen in that setting. Practice coming up with story ideas by listing four interesting events that could happen in each setting below.

1. Setting: an attic filled with old boxes

   Someone could find an old box with a strange machine in it.

   _____

   _____

   _____

2. Setting: a cave hidden behind a waterfall

   _____

   _____

   _____

   _____

3. Setting: an old zoo that has closed down

   _____

   _____

   _____

   _____

Set 3: Understanding Setting

Writing Prompt 11

The setting of a story is where and when a story takes place. You will sometimes be asked to write a story with a given setting. Read the writing prompt below.

> Write a story that takes place at a train station in the middle of the day.

The writing prompt tells you where the events of the story will take place. You have to decide what the events will be. Start by thinking about things that could happen in that setting. Think about what the setting would be like. In the middle of the day, the train station would probably be very busy. You can use this detail in your story. You can also decide on a character for your story.

The table shows a plan for a story set in a busy train station. Use the plan below to write a story. Write or type a story of about 1 page.

The Beginning: Introduce the setting and the main character.
Margo is waiting for the train with her little brother Sam. There are people everywhere.
→ Start your story by writing a paragraph that describes where the main character is and what the main character is doing.
The Middle: Describe the interesting or exciting event that happens.
Margo loses Sam. She stands on a bench to try and spot him. She starts to call out his name.
→ Write two or three paragraphs that describe these events.
The Ending: Describe what happens in the end.
Sam yells out to tell Margo to be quiet. She turns around and sees that he is napping on a bench right behind her.
→End your story by writing a paragraph that describes these events.

Writing Prompt 12

Write a story that takes place in a school library.

Start by thinking of story ideas. Think of interesting or exciting things that could happen in a school library. Then choose the idea you want to base your story on.

Use the table below to plan your story. Write or type a story of about 1 page.

The Beginning: Introduce the setting and the main character. → **Start your story by writing a paragraph that describes where the main character is and what the main character is doing.**
The Middle: Describe the interesting or exciting event that happens. → **Write two or three paragraphs that describe these events.**
The Ending: Describe what happens in the end. →**End your story by writing a paragraph that describes these events.**

Writing Prompt 13

Write a story that takes place in the setting shown below.

Use the table below to plan your story. Write or type a story of about 1 page.

The Beginning: Introduce the setting and the main character.   **→ Start your story by writing a paragraph that describes where the main character is and what the main character is doing.**
The Middle: Describe the interesting or exciting event that happens.   **→ Write two or three paragraphs that describe these events.**
The Ending: Describe what happens in the end.   **→End your story by writing a paragraph that describes these events.**

Writing Prompt 14

Write a story that takes place at the top of a tall tower.

Start by thinking of story ideas. Think of interesting or exciting things that could happen at the top of a tall tower. Then choose the idea you want to base your story on.

Use the table below to plan your story. Write or type a story of about 1 page.

The Beginning: Introduce the setting and the main character.   → **Start your story by writing a paragraph that describes where the main character is and what the main character is doing.**
The Middle: Describe the interesting or exciting event that happens.   → **Write two or three paragraphs that describe these events.**
The Ending: Describe what happens in the end.   →**End your story by writing a paragraph that describes these events.**

Writing Prompt 15

Write a story that takes place on a baseball field at night.

Start by thinking of story ideas. Think of interesting or exciting things that could happen on the baseball field. Think about who might be at the baseball field at night and why. Then choose the idea you want to base your story on.

Use the table below to plan your story. Write or type a story of about 1 page.

The Beginning: Introduce the setting and the main character.   → **Start your story by writing a paragraph that describes where the main character is and what the main character is doing.**
The Middle: Describe the interesting or exciting event that happens.   → **Write two or three paragraphs that describe these events.**
The Ending: Describe what happens in the end.   →**End your story by writing a paragraph that describes these events.**

Warm-Up Exercise: Characters Traits and Problems

In the next set, you will learn about main characters. You will need to think about what characters are like. Many stories are based on problems that occur because of what the character is like. Complete the table by adding a problem that each character might have.

Character	Problem
a shy girl	*finds it hard to make friends at a new school*
an honest boy	*makes his sister mad when he says her art is bad*
a curious boy	
a bossy sister	
a lazy man	
a daring boy	
a sneaky girl	
a loud grandpa	
a grumpy uncle	

Set 4: Creating a Main Character

Writing Prompt 16

The main character of a story is who the story is mainly about. When writing a story, it is important to think about who the main character is and what the main character is like. The events of the story can be based around what the character is like. Read the description of the character Darius below.

Darius is very clumsy. He is always dropping things.

Think about what a story about Darius could be about. What could happen because of how clumsy he is? What problem could someone who is clumsy face?

The table below shows the plan for a story about Darius. Use the plan below to write a story. Write or type a story of about 1 page.

The Beginning: Introduce the main character.
Darius has really long arms and legs. He is a fast runner, but he is very clumsy. He is always dropping things.
→ Start your story by writing a paragraph that tells who the main character is and what the main character is like.
The Middle: Describe what happens because of what the character is like.
Darius is the fastest runner on the track team, so he goes last in the relay. He grabs the baton. He is in the lead. Then it flies out of his hand. He crosses the line first, but it does not count.
→ Write two or three paragraphs that describe these events.
The Ending: Describe what the character does in the end, how the character feels, or how the character changes.
Darius is upset. Darius feels bad for letting his team down.
→Write a paragraph that concludes the story.

Writing Prompt 17

Write a story about the character described below.

A fireman who is scared of heights.

Think about an interesting event that occurs because of what the character is like. Use the table below to plan your story. Write or type a story of about 1 page.

The Beginning: Introduce the main character.   → Start your story by writing a paragraph that tells who the main character is and what the main character is like.
The Middle: Describe what happens because of what the character is like.   → Write two or three paragraphs that describe these events.
The Ending: Describe what the character does in the end, how the character feels, or how the character changes.   →Write a paragraph that concludes the story.

Narrative Writing Workbook, Grade 4

Writing Prompt 18

Write a story about the character shown in the picture below. You can choose what she is like. Maybe she could be greedy, bossy, or mean. What might happen because of what she is like? Use this to come up with a story idea.

Use the table below to plan your story. Write or type a story of about 1 page.

The Beginning: Introduce the main character.   → Start your story by writing a paragraph that tells who the main character is and what the main character is like.
The Middle: Describe what happens because of what the character is like.   → Write two or three paragraphs that describe these events.
The Ending: Describe what the character does in the end, how the character feels, or how the character changes.   →Write a paragraph that concludes the story.

Writing Prompt 19

The characters in a story do not have to be people. Many stories have animals as characters. Write a story where the main character is a lonely polar bear.

Use the table below to plan your story. Write or type a story of about 1 page.

The Beginning: Introduce the main character.
→ **Start your story by writing a paragraph that tells who the main character is and what the main character is like.**
The Middle: Describe what happens because of what the character is like.
→ Write two or three paragraphs that describe these events.
The Ending: Describe what the character does in the end, how the character feels, or how the character changes.
→Write a paragraph that concludes the story.

Writing Prompt 20

Write a story about the character described below.

A waiter who loses his temper.

Use the table below to plan your story. Write or type a story of about 1 page.

The Beginning: Introduce the main character.   → **Start your story by writing a paragraph that tells who the main character is and what the main character is like.**
The Middle: Describe what happens because of what the character is like.   → Write two or three paragraphs that describe these events.
The Ending: Describe what the character does in the end, how the character feels, or how the character changes.   →Write a paragraph that concludes the story.

Warm-Up Exercise: Using Details to Show Feelings

In the next set, you will use descriptions to show how characters feel. The feelings of characters are often important parts of stories. Stories do not need to state how a character feels. It is better to give details that show how the character feels. Read the two examples below.

> Kevin tried to stay awake, but he felt very tired.

> Kevin yawned and rubbed his eyes. He told himself he would close his eyes just for a minute.

The first example states that Kevin is tired. The second example is better because it shows that Kevin is tired. Now practice using details to show how characters feel by listing four actions that show how each character feels.

1. Lawrence is excited when he wins a running race.

   He clapped his hands together.

   _____

   _____

   _____

2. Jessica is nervous as she waits to hear if the new baby is a brother or a sister.

   Jessica wiped some sweat from her forehead.

   _____

   _____

   _____

3 Randy wakes up in the morning feeling grumpy.

_____

_____

_____

_____

4 Ella is startled when her brother leaps out of her closet to scare her.

_____

_____

_____

_____

Choose one of the characters above. Use the actions you listed to write a paragraph that shows how the character feels.

_____

_____

_____

_____

_____

Set 5: Using Descriptions

Writing Prompt 21

Stories often need to show how characters feel. Good writers do not state how characters feel. They use descriptions to show how characters feel. Read the first paragraph from a short story on the next page.

The paragraph does not state how Deepak feels, but you can tell by his actions that he feels excited.

The table below shows the plan for a story about Deepak. Use the plan below to complete the story. Be sure to use descriptions to show how Deepak feels during the story. Write your story on the next page.

The Beginning: Describe how the character feels at first.
Deepak gets home from school. He is excited to tell his parents that his school is planning a trip to Mexico City.
→ This part has already been done for you. The first paragraph introduces the main character and shows how the main character feels.
The Middle: Describe what happens to change how the character feels.
Deepak tells his parents about the trip. His parents say they are not sure it sounds like a good idea. They want to speak to the school.
→ Write two or three paragraphs that describe these events.
The Ending: Describe how the character feels in the end.
Deepak is worried. He hopes that his parents will let him go.
→Write a paragraph that describes how the character feels now. You can use descriptions to show how the character feels.

Mexico City

Deepak raced down the driveway and burst through the front door. He ran from room to room looking for his parents. He had great news to tell them. His school was planning a trip to Mexico City.

Writing Prompt 22

Write a story about the character described below. Use descriptions to show how the character feels.

Jamie is stuck inside on a rainy Sunday.

Use the table below to plan your story. Write or type a story of about 1 page.

The Beginning: Describe how the character feels at first.   → **Start your story by writing a paragraph that introduces the main character and shows how the main character feels.**
The Middle: Describe what happens to change how the character feels.   → **Write two or three paragraphs that describe these events.**
The Ending: Describe how the character feels in the end.   →**Write a paragraph that describes how the character feels now. You can use descriptions to show how the character feels.**

Writing Prompt 23

Write a story about the character described below. Use descriptions to show how the character feels.

Salma is about to perform a song in front of a crowd.

Use the table below to plan your story. Write or type a story of about 1 page.

The Beginning: Describe how the character feels at first.
→ Start your story by writing a paragraph that introduces the main character and shows how the main character feels.
The Middle: Describe what happens to change how the character feels.
→ Write two or three paragraphs that describe these events.
The Ending: Describe how the character feels in the end.
→Write a paragraph that describes how the character feels now. You can use descriptions to show how the character feels.

Writing Prompt 24

Write a story about the character described below. Use descriptions to show how the character feels.

Louis must walk through a swamp that could be home to snakes.

Use the table below to plan your story. Write or type a story of about 1 page.

The Beginning: Describe how the character feels at first.   → **Start your story by writing a paragraph that introduces the main character and shows how the main character feels.**
The Middle: Describe what happens to change how the character feels.   → **Write two or three paragraphs that describe these events.**
The Ending: Describe how the character feels in the end.   →**Write a paragraph that describes how the character feels now. You can use descriptions to show how the character feels.**

Writing Prompt 25

Write a story about the character described below. Use descriptions to show how the character feels.

> Chandra had never babysat on her own before. She hoped that everything would go well.

Use the table below to plan your story. Write or type a story of about 1 page.

The Beginning: Describe how the character feels at first.   → Start your story by writing a paragraph that introduces the main character and shows how the main character feels.
The Middle: Describe what happens to change how the character feels.   → Write two or three paragraphs that describe these events.
The Ending: Describe how the character feels in the end.   →Write a paragraph that describes how the character feels now. You can use descriptions to show how the character feels.

Set 6: Using Dialogue

Writing Prompt 26

Dialogue are words spoken by characters. Read the start of a story on the next page.

The words spoken by the characters show you what is happening in the story. You can tell that Hoy is used to riding horses. You can guess that Ellen has never ridden a horse before. You can also guess that Ellen feels a bit scared.

The table below shows a story a student planned that started with this dialogue. Use the plan below to write a story. Write your story on the next page.

The Beginning: Describe what happens first.
Hoy invites Ellen to go horse riding. Ellen feels unsure.
→ **This part has already been done for you. The first paragraph tells who the story is about and what is happening.**
The Middle: Describe what happens next.
Ellen decides to try it. Then Ellen's horse takes off. She is taken on a wild ride. Hoy chases Ellen and tries to calm Ellen's horse.
→ **Continue the story by telling what happens. You can use dialogue and descriptions to show what is happening or how characters feel.**
The Ending: Describe what happens in the end.
Ellen's horse finally stops. She will not get back on. They walk the horses back to the stables.
→ **End your story by telling what happens. You can use dialogue and descriptions to show what is happening or how characters feel.**

A Wild Ride

"Riding a horse is easy," Hoy said.

Ellen looked at the horse for a long time.

"I don't know about this," she said. "He looks kind of scary."

Writing Prompt 27

Write a story that begins with the sentence below.

"Do you think the water in the creek is safe to drink?" Kieran asked.

Start by thinking about what could be happening in the story. Where could Kieran be? What could he be doing? Why is he thinking about drinking water out of a creek? What might happen if he drinks the water?

Use the table below to plan your story. Write or type a story of about 1 page.

The Beginning: Describe what happens first.   → **Start your story by telling who the story is about and what is happening.**
The Middle: Describe what happens next.   → **Continue the story by telling what happens. You can use dialogue and descriptions to show what is happening or how characters feel.**
The Ending: Describe what happens in the end.   → **End your story by telling what happens. You can use dialogue and descriptions to show what is happening or how characters feel.**

Writing Prompt 28

Write a story that begins with the sentence below.

"Have you seen a small white dog with a green collar?" Emma asked.

Use the table below to plan your story. Write or type a story of about 1 page.

The Beginning: Describe what happens first.   → **Start your story by telling who the story is about and what is happening.**
The Middle: Describe what happens next.   → **Continue the story by telling what happens. You can use dialogue and descriptions to show what is happening or how characters feel.**
The Ending: Describe what happens in the end.   → **End your story by telling what happens. You can use dialogue and descriptions to show what is happening or how characters feel.**

Writing Prompt 29

Imagine that two good friends are having a fight. Write a story about the fight. Use at least two lines of dialogue in your story.

Use the table below to plan your story. Write or type a story of about 1 page.

The Beginning: Describe what happens first.   → **Start your story by telling who the story is about and what is happening.**
The Middle: Describe what happens next.   → **Continue the story by telling what happens. You can use dialogue and descriptions to show what is happening or how characters feel.**
The Ending: Describe what happens in the end.   → **End your story by telling what happens. You can use dialogue and descriptions to show what is happening or how characters feel.**

Writing Prompt 30

Janet cannot find her shoe. She decides that she has to find out where her shoe has gone. Write a story about Janet's search for her missing shoe. Use at least two lines of dialogue in your story.

Use the table below to plan your story. Write or type a story of about 1 page.

The Beginning: Describe what happens first.   → Start your story by telling who the story is about and what is happening.
The Middle: Describe what happens next.   → Continue the story by telling what happens. You can use dialogue and descriptions to show what is happening or how characters feel.
The Ending: Describe what happens in the end.   → End your story by telling what happens. You can use dialogue and descriptions to show what is happening or how characters feel.

Warm-Up Exercise: Characters Learning Lessons

In the next set, you will write stories on given themes. You will learn that a story's theme often comes from a lesson a character learns. For example, a story might have a theme about being honest. The story could show the theme by describing a person who gets caught lying and learns why it is important to be honest.

Now practice thinking about lessons learned. Complete each diagram to show how the character learns the lesson. The first one has been completed for you.

1 Jason learns that practice makes perfect.

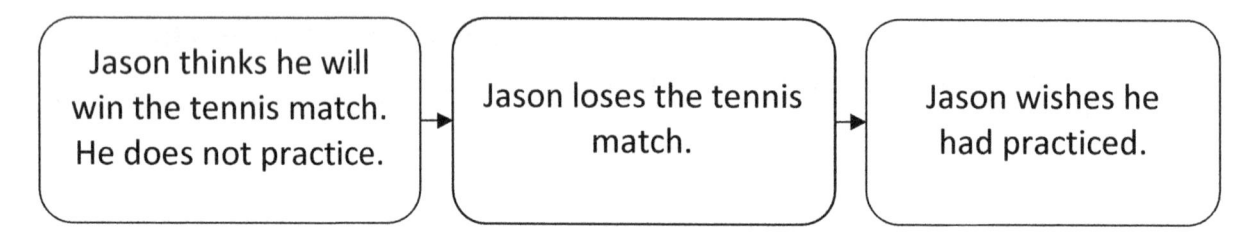

| Jason thinks he will win the tennis match. He does not practice. | → | Jason loses the tennis match. | → | Jason wishes he had practiced. |

2 Sue learns to be patient.

| Sue puts a cake in the oven. She doesn't want to wait an hour to taste it. | → | | → | |

3 Louis learns not to judge people too quickly.

| Louis thinks the new boy on the basketball team will be no good because he is short. | → | | → | |

Set 7: Understanding Theme

Writing Prompt 31

The theme of a story is an important idea in the story. It is often a lesson that the story teaches, or a lesson a character learns in the story. Read the theme below.

It is important to be a good sport.

Think about what could happen in a story to teach this lesson. Remember that the story does not have to state the lesson. Instead, readers learn the lesson by what happens in the story. Think about different ways that someone could learn that it is important to be a good sport.

The table below shows a story a student planned with this theme. Use the plan below to write a story. Write or type a story of about 1 page.

The Beginning: Introduce the main character and show what he or she is like.
Leo's team wins their first baseball game easily. Leo makes fun of the players on the other team.
→ Start your story by showing what the main character is like and what is happening.
The Middle: Describe what happens to teach the character a lesson.
In the next game, Leo's team loses when Leo misses a catch. Another player laughs at Leo and teases him about it.
→ Write two or three paragraphs that describe these events.
The Ending: Describe how the character has learned a lesson.
Leo realizes that it does not feel good to lose and be made fun of. He decides he will be nicer to the other players next time he wins.
→ Write a paragraph that shows how the character has changed.

Writing Prompt 32

Write a story that describes how someone learns to work better with other people.

Start by thinking of a situation where someone tries to work alone but it does not work. Use this situation to come up with your story idea.

Use the table below to plan your story. Write or type a story of about 1 page.

The Beginning: Introduce the main character and show what he or she is like.   → **Start your story by showing what the main character is like and what is happening.**
The Middle: Describe what happens to teach the character a lesson.   → **Write two or three paragraphs that describe these events.**
The Ending: Describe how the character has learned a lesson.   → **Write a paragraph that shows how the character has changed.**

Writing Prompt 33

Write a story with the message below.

Do not be afraid to speak your mind.

Start by thinking of what might happen to teach a character to say what they think instead of keeping quiet. Choose one set of events that would teach someone the lesson.

Use the table below to plan your story. Write or type a story of about 1 page.

The Beginning: Introduce the main character and show what he or she is like.   → **Start your story by showing what the main character is like and what is happening.**
The Middle: Describe what happens to teach the character a lesson.   → **Write two or three paragraphs that describe these events.**
The Ending: Describe how the character has learned a lesson.   → **Write a paragraph that shows how the character has changed.**

Writing Prompt 34

Write a story with the message below.

> If something is worth doing, it is worth doing well.

Start by thinking of a situation where someone does something quickly instead of doing it right. Use this situation to come up with your story idea.

Use the table below to plan your story. Write or type a story of about 1 page.

The Beginning: Introduce the main character and show what he or she is like.   → **Start your story by showing what the main character is like and what is happening.**
The Middle: Describe what happens to teach the character a lesson.   → **Write two or three paragraphs that describe these events.**
The Ending: Describe how the character has learned a lesson.   → **Write a paragraph that shows how the character has changed.**

Writing Prompt 35

The title of a story sometimes tells what the theme of the story is. Write a story with the title below.

The Best Things in Life are Free

Start by thinking about what might happen to teach someone the lesson described in the title. Choose one set of events to use as your story idea.

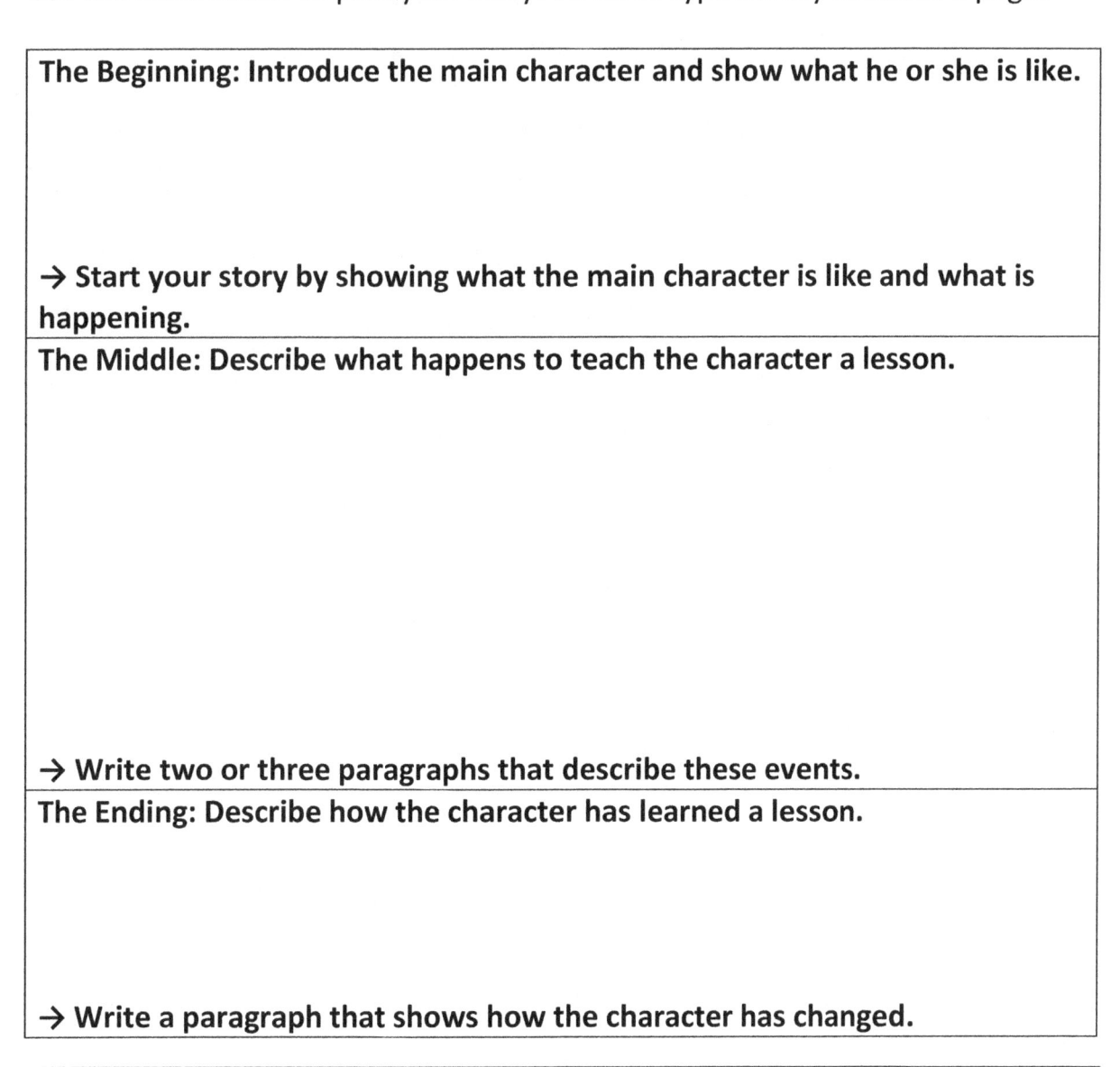

Use the table below to plan your story. Write or type a story of about 1 page.

The Beginning: Introduce the main character and show what he or she is like.   → **Start your story by showing what the main character is like and what is happening.**
The Middle: Describe what happens to teach the character a lesson.   → **Write two or three paragraphs that describe these events.**
The Ending: Describe how the character has learned a lesson.   → **Write a paragraph that shows how the character has changed.**

Set 8: Starting Strong

Writing Prompt 36

The opening of a story is very important. It often introduces the character, the setting, and the main problem. It tells the reader who the story is about and what is happening. Read the first sentences from a story on the next page.

These sentences show three things:
- The main character is a star basketball player named Mike.
- The setting is the last minute of a basketball game.
- The main problem is that Mike wants his team to win.

The table below shows a plan for a story that started with these sentences. Use the plan below to complete the story. Write your story on the next page.

The Beginning: Introduce the main character, the setting, and the problem.
Mike is a star basketball player. His team is behind. He wants his team to win.
→ **This part has been done for you. It tells the character, setting, and problem.**
The Middle: Describe what the character does to solve the problem.
Mike gathers his teammates and talks about doing their best. They tell him they will do whatever it takes. Mike tells them the plan. He will get the ball in the last second to take the final shot.
→ **Write two or three paragraphs that describe these events.**
The Ending: Describe what happens in the end. You might show how the problem is solved or how the character feels.
Mike's teammates carry out the plan. Mike gets the ball. He scores the winning basket with a second to go.
→**End your story by writing a paragraph that shows that the problem is solved.**

Playing to Win

There was less than a minute left of the game. Mike was the captain of the team. He was also the star player. He had to get his team to win.

Writing Prompt 37

Write a story that begins with the sentences on the next page.

Use the table below to plan your story. Write your story on the next page.

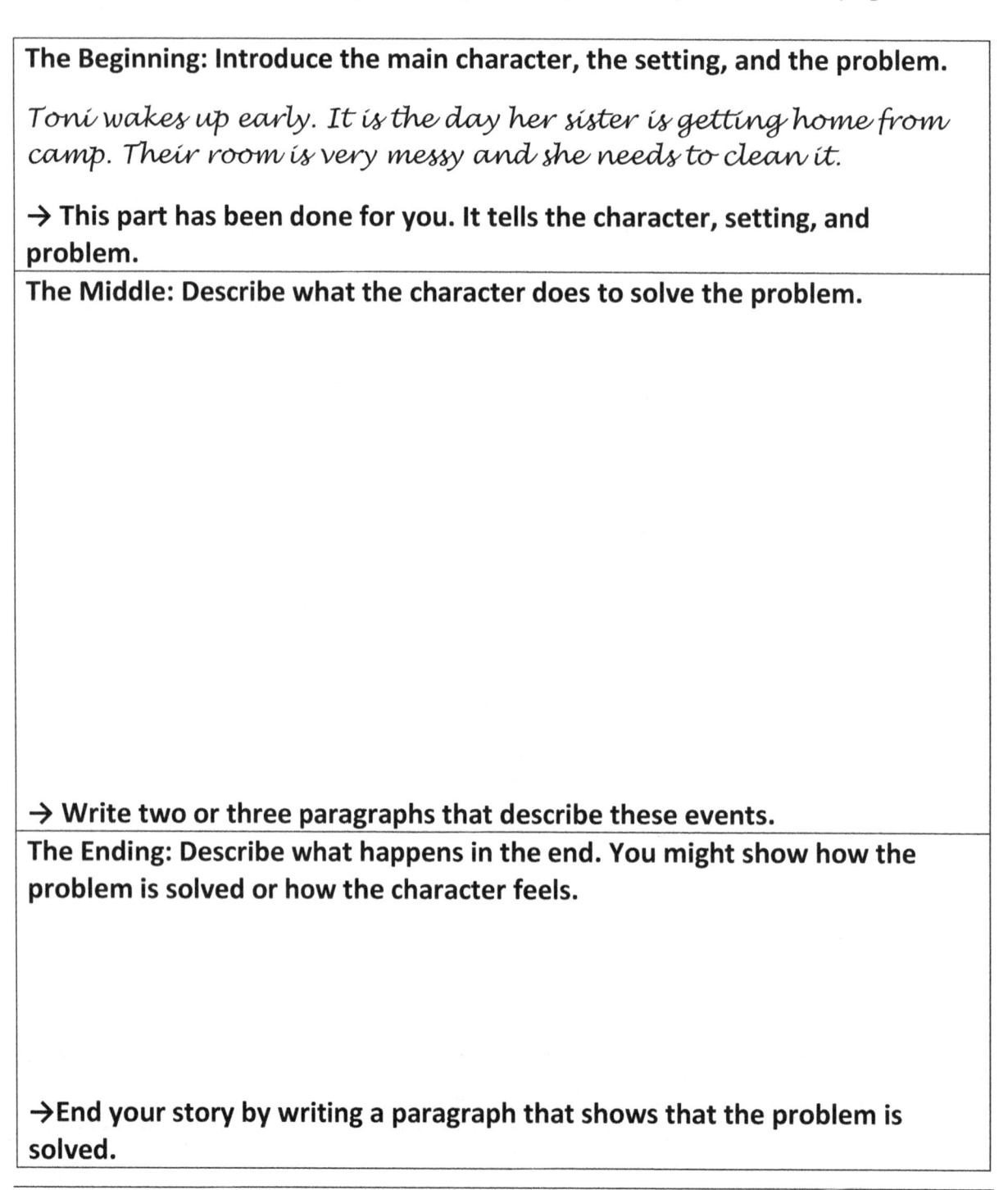

The Beginning: Introduce the main character, the setting, and the problem.   *Toni wakes up early. It is the day her sister is getting home from camp. Their room is very messy and she needs to clean it.*   → **This part has been done for you. It tells the character, setting, and problem.**
The Middle: Describe what the character does to solve the problem.   → **Write two or three paragraphs that describe these events.**
The Ending: Describe what happens in the end. You might show how the problem is solved or how the character feels.   →**End your story by writing a paragraph that shows that the problem is solved.**

Quick Clean-Up

Toni opened her eyes and yawned. Then she remembered what day it was. It was the day her sister was getting home from camp. She knew her sister would be mad if she saw how messy their room was.

Writing Prompt 38

Write a story that begins with the sentences on the next page.

Use the table below to plan your story. Write your story on the next page.

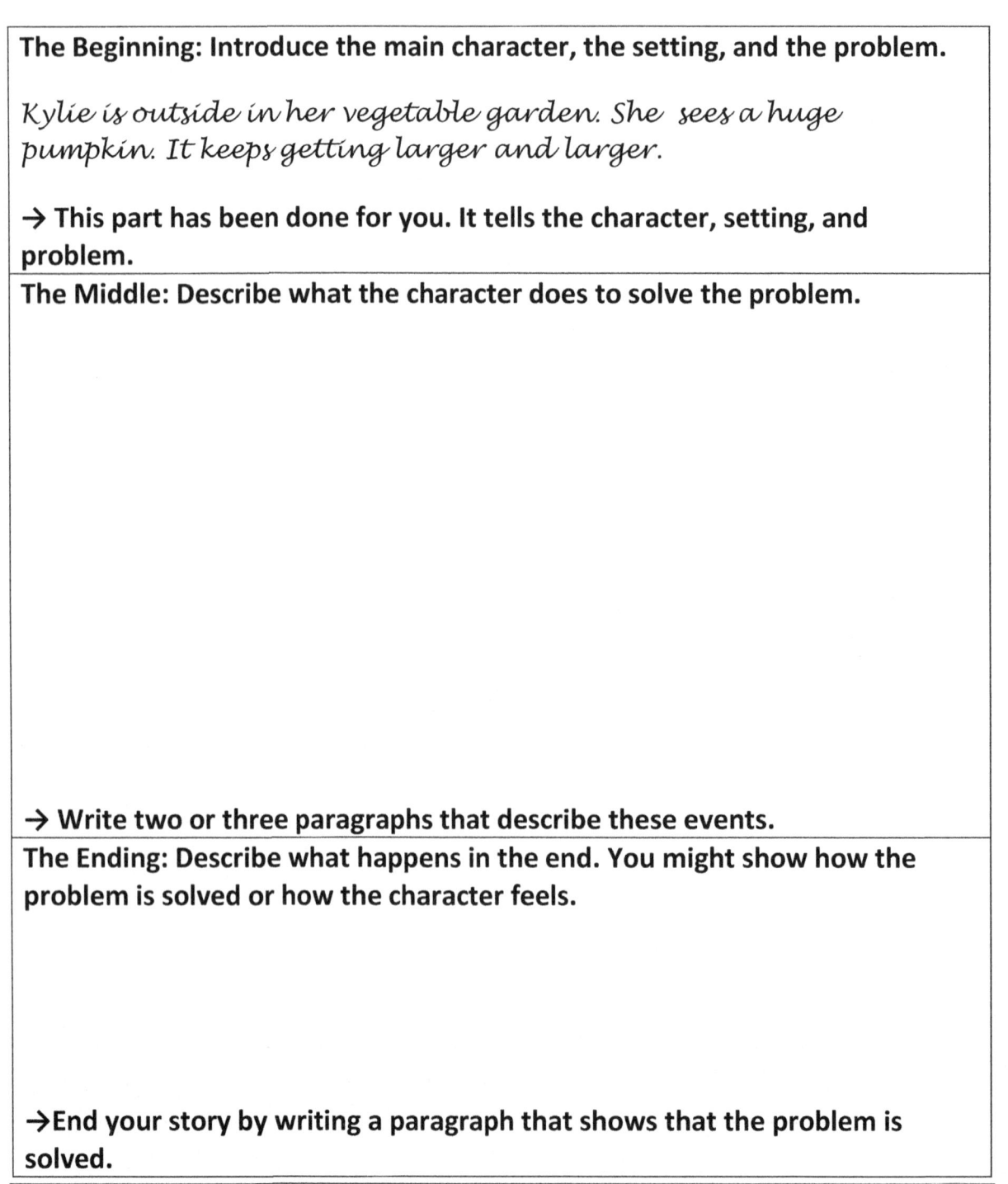

The Beginning: Introduce the main character, the setting, and the problem. *Kylie is outside in her vegetable garden. She sees a huge pumpkin. It keeps getting larger and larger.* → **This part has been done for you. It tells the character, setting, and problem.**
The Middle: Describe what the character does to solve the problem.   → **Write two or three paragraphs that describe these events.**
The Ending: Describe what happens in the end. You might show how the problem is solved or how the character feels.   →**End your story by writing a paragraph that shows that the problem is solved.**

The Giant Growing Pumpkin

Kylie walked out into the vegetable garden. She was amazed when she saw the size of the pumpkin. It was huge. As she watched, it grew even larger. It would soon fill the whole garden.

Writing Prompt 39

Write a story that begins with the event below. Be sure to introduce the character, setting, and problem in the first paragraph.

> Alison is tiptoeing to the bathroom late one night when she knocks over and breaks her mother's favorite vase.

Use the table below to plan your story. Write or type a story of about 1 page.

The Beginning: Introduce the main character, the setting, and the problem.   → Start your story by writing a paragraph that shows who the story is about, where the events take place, and what the main problem is.
The Middle: Describe what the character does to solve the problem.   → Write two or three paragraphs that describe these events.
The Ending: Describe what happens in the end. You might show how the problem is solved or how the character feels.   →End your story by writing a paragraph that shows that the problem is solved.

Writing Prompt 40

Write a story that begins with the event below. Be sure to introduce the character, setting, and problem in the first paragraph.

> Ryan is riding to school. He is already running late when his bike gets a flat tire.

Use the table below to plan your story. Write or type a story of about 1 page.

The Beginning: Introduce the main character, the setting, and the problem.   → Start your story by writing a paragraph that shows who the story is about, where the events take place, and what the main problem is.
The Middle: Describe what the character does to solve the problem.   → Write two or three paragraphs that describe these events.
The Ending: Describe what happens in the end. You might show how the problem is solved or how the character feels.   →End your story by writing a paragraph that shows that the problem is solved.

Warm-Up Exercise: Choosing Descriptive Words

In the next sets, you will learn about using details to describe things. The words you use to describe things are called adjectives. You can improve your writing by choosing strong adjectives that tell a lot about what you are describing. Read the sentences below.

The big castle sat on top of a tall mountain.
The giant castle sat on top of a towering mountain.

The second sentence has stronger adjectives. They more clearly show what the castle and mountain are like. Now practice using strong words by replacing the underlined word in each sentence with a stronger one.

1 The soup tasted so bad that I spat it out.

   The soup tasted so _____ that I spat it out.

2 The boys were shaking when they got out of the cold water.

   The boys were shaking when they got out of the _____ water.

3 The loud music woke Michael from his sleep.

   The _____ music woke Michael from his sleep.

4 The kittens were small when they were born.

   The kittens were _____ when they were born.

5 Max looked up at the large ship resting on the water.

   Max looked up at the _____ ship resting on the water.

Warm-Up Exercise: Choosing Action Words

The words you use to describe actions are called verbs. You can improve your writing by choosing strong verbs. A strong verb might suggest how something is done or how the person doing it feels. Read the sentences below.

Charlie <u>lay</u> down on the bed and fell asleep right away.
Charlie <u>flopped</u> down on the bed and fell asleep right away.

The word *flopped* is stronger than *lay* because it shows how Charlie lay down and suggests he is tired. Now practice using strong words by replacing the underlined word in each sentence with a stronger one.

1. Zoe was so mad that she <u>walked</u> out of the room.

   Zoe was so mad that she _____ out of the room.

2. Sammy jumped on his bike and <u>rode</u> down the hill.

   Sammy jumped on his bike and _____ down the hill.

3. I <u>looked</u> at the amazing view for a long time.

   I _____ at the amazing view for a long time.

4. Antonio <u>threw</u> the football as far as he could.

   Antonio _____ the football as far as he could.

5. Kim <u>held</u> onto the edge of the cliff with her fingertips.

   Kim _____ onto the edge of the cliff with her fingertips.

Set 9: Using Concrete Details

When writing stories, concrete details can make your writing come alive. Concrete details are specific details. Read the description below.

> The rain fell hard. Rose tried to use her old umbrella to keep dry. The rain was too heavy for it. Rose got very wet.

The description of the rain and what Rose does is vague. Now read the description below.

> The large raindrops slammed down into the ground. Rose's flimsy old umbrella was no match for it. Rose held it down close to her head and tried to huddle under it, but it was no use. She was soaked through in seconds.

This paragraph uses specific details. You can imagine how hard the rain is falling. You can imagine how Rose is trying to stay dry, and how cold she feels. The second paragraph uses concrete details in several ways. Here are some tips for using concrete details.

Using Concrete Details

Tip	Example
Use good descriptive words.	It is better to describe the "flimsy old umbrella" than just the "old umbrella."
Use good action words.	It is better to say that the "raindrops slammed down" than that the "rain fell hard."
Use images.	The image of Rose holding the umbrella close to her head shows how she is trying hard to stay dry.
Describe specific actions.	The description of how Rose "huddled under" her umbrella shows that she is trying to stay dry, and suggests that she is cold.

Now practice using concrete details by completing the exercises.

Writing Prompt 41

Imagine that you are at the beach watching a large storm. List four concrete details about the storm. The first one has been completed for you.

1. *The waves slammed against the rocks.*

2. _____

_____

3. _____

_____

4. _____

_____

Use the details to write a paragraph describing the storm.

_____

_____

_____

_____

_____

_____

Writing Prompt 42

Imagine you are looking at a very messy kitchen after your younger sisters have tried to bake a cake. Write four concrete details about the kitchen. The first one has been completed for you.

1. *Dark chocolate batter dripped down onto the kitchen floor.*

2. _____

_____

3. _____

_____

4. _____

_____

Use the details to write a paragraph describing the messy kitchen.

_____

_____

_____

_____

_____

_____

Writing Prompt 43

Imagine you have gone skydiving, and you are just about to jump out of the plane. Write four concrete details about how scared you feel. The first one has been completed for you.

1. *My hands held the straps so tightly that my knuckles were white.*

2. _____

3. _____

4. _____

Use the details to write a paragraph describing how scared you feel.

_____

Writing Prompt 44

Read this paragraph a student wrote about a concert they went to.

> The music was amazing. The band played some great songs. I had a really good time. I will never forget it.

The paragraph is vague and does not use concrete details. Now imagine that you have just been to a great concert. Write a paragraph or two describing how great the concert was. Be sure to use concrete details.

_____

_____

_____

_____

_____

_____

_____

_____

_____

Writing Prompt 45

Read this paragraph a student wrote about seeing an old friend again.

> I was so excited to see Kasey again. I had not seen her for a long time. I had been looking forward to seeing her for ages.

The paragraph is vague and does not use concrete details. Now imagine that you are waiting to see an old friend. Write a paragraph or two describing how you feel about seeing your friend again. Be sure to use concrete details.

_____

_____

_____

_____

_____

_____

_____

_____

_____

_____

Set 10: Using Sensory Details

Sensory details are details that describe what things look like, taste like, smell like, sound like, or feel like. Sensory details help readers imagine what you are describing. Read this paragraph about a busy newspaper office.

> Young workers rushed from one end of the office to the other. Some were carrying papers. Others were carrying stacks of books. They seemed to be hurrying everywhere they went. Workers at their desks were typing quickly. You could hear the quick tapping of keys. Other workers whispered to each other in excited voices.

This paragraph describes things you see in the office, such as the workers rushing around carrying papers and books. It also describes the sound of the office. The paragraph does not state that the office is busy, but you can tell by the details that it is. The paragraph does not state what is happening, but you can guess that everyone is excited about something. This paragraph shows how sensory details can make a scene come alive.

This paragraph uses the senses of sight and sound. There are five senses that can be used when writing stories. The table below describes each sense. When adding sensory details, you can choose to focus on one or more of the senses. The senses you use will depend on what you are writing about.

The Five Senses

Sense	Details to Include
sight	what can be seen
hearing	what sounds are heard
smell	what things smell like
taste	what things taste like
touch	what things feel like

Now practice using sensory details by completing the exercises.

Writing Prompt 46

Imagine you are walking along a beach on a hot summer day.

Describe the feel of the warm sand.

_____

_____

_____

_____

Describe the sound of the crashing waves.

_____

_____

_____

_____

Describe how the beach smells.

_____

_____

_____

_____

Writing Prompt 47

Think of a food that is delicious. Describe the taste of the food.

_____

_____

_____

_____

_____

_____

Think of a food that is horrible. Describe the taste of the food.

_____

_____

_____

_____

_____

_____

Writing Prompt 48

Imagine you are in a classroom taking a test. Describe the sound of the classroom.

___

Imagine you are sitting in a stadium watching a football game. Describe the sound of the crowd.

Writing Prompt 49

Imagine you are watching a volcano erupt. Describe what you see.

_____

_____

_____

_____

_____

_____

Imagine you look out the window after it has been snowing all night. Describe what you see.

_____

_____

_____

_____

_____

_____

Writing Prompt 50

Use sensory details to describe the animal below. Include what the animal looks like and what the animal would feel like.

___
___
___
___
___
___
___
___

Set 11: Using a Narrator

Writing Prompt 51

Stories have different points of view. A story with a first-person point of view has a narrator telling the story. Narrators describe the events as if they are happening to them. Read the first few sentences of a story on the next page.

The narrator of the story is a person who has lost her younger brother in a shopping mall. One benefit of writing in first-person is that you can have narrators describe their feelings. In this story, you can describe how the narrator feels worried at the start. Then you can describe how the narrator feels thankful once she finds her brother.

The table below shows the plan for a story about the search for the missing boy. The plan is also written in first-person point of view. Use the plan below to complete the story. Write your story on the next page.

The Beginning: Describe what is happening and how the narrator feels.
I was in a shopping center when I lost my brother Felix. I was very worried as soon as I realized he was missing.
→ This part has already been done for you. The first paragraph introduces the narrator and shows how the narrator feels.
The Middle: Describe what happens next.
I started calling his name. A lady asked me what was wrong, and then she started calling out too. More people joined in.
→ Write two or three paragraphs that describe these events.
The Ending: Describe what happens in the end and how the narrator feels.
Felix came running out of a pet store. I felt very glad to see him.
→Write a paragraph that tells what happens in the end and shows how the narrator feels.

Finding Felix

I spun around and looked in every direction. My little brother Felix had been with me a second ago. Now he was nowhere to be seen in the busy shopping mall. There were dozens of shops he could be in. I took a deep breath and tried to stay calm.

_____

_____

_____

_____

_____

_____

_____

_____

_____

_____

_____

_____

_____

_____

Writing Prompt 52

Write a story about a girl who gets an "F" on a test when she usually gets good grades. Write your story from the point of view of the girl.

Use the table below to plan your story. Write or type a story of about 1 page.

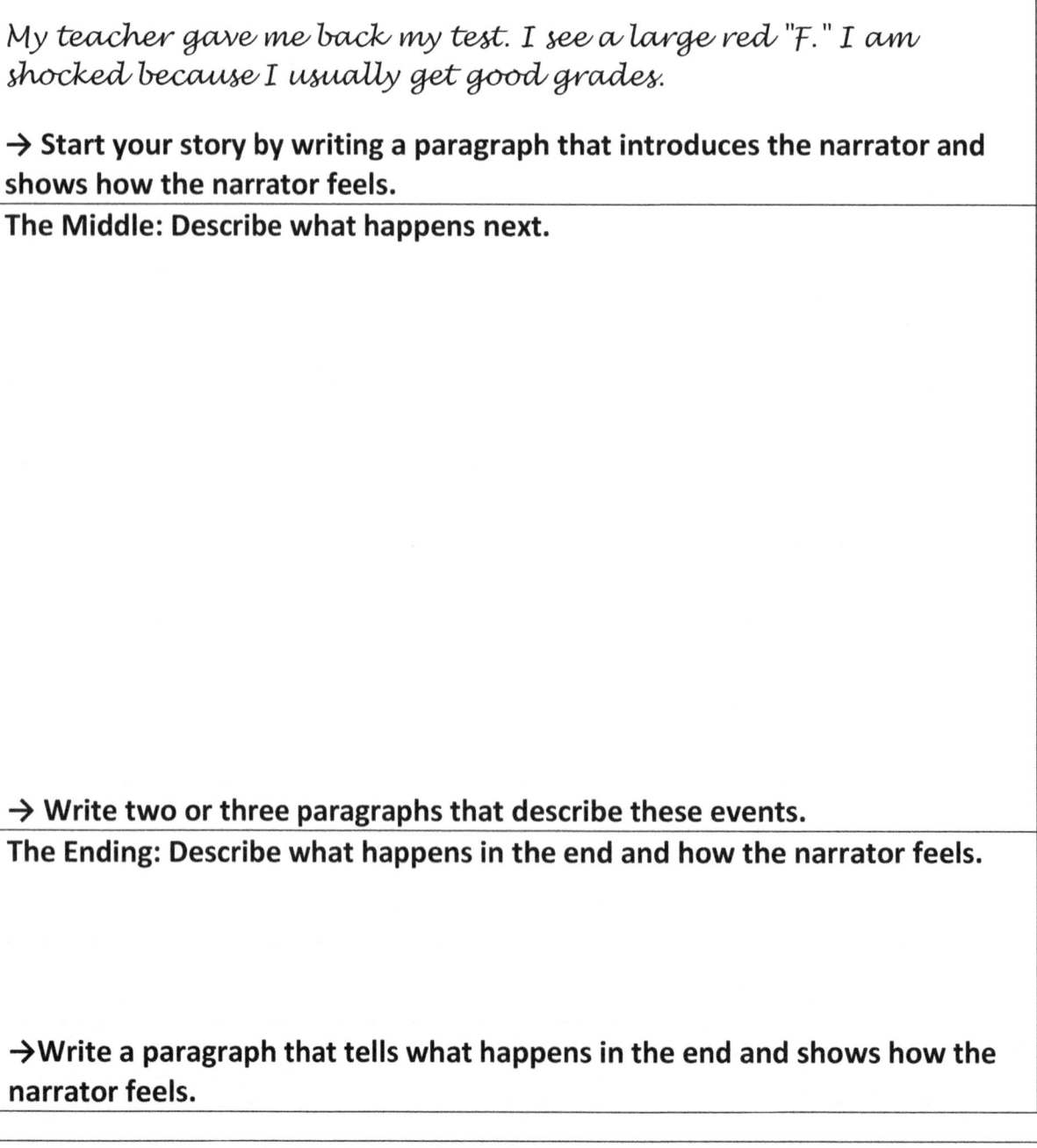

The Beginning: Describe what is happening and how the narrator feels.   *My teacher gave me back my test. I see a large red "F." I am shocked because I usually get good grades.*   → **Start your story by writing a paragraph that introduces the narrator and shows how the narrator feels.**
The Middle: Describe what happens next.   → **Write two or three paragraphs that describe these events.**
The Ending: Describe what happens in the end and how the narrator feels.   →**Write a paragraph that tells what happens in the end and shows how the narrator feels.**

Writing Prompt 53

Write a story from the point of view of a ghost who has people move into the house he has lived in alone for years.

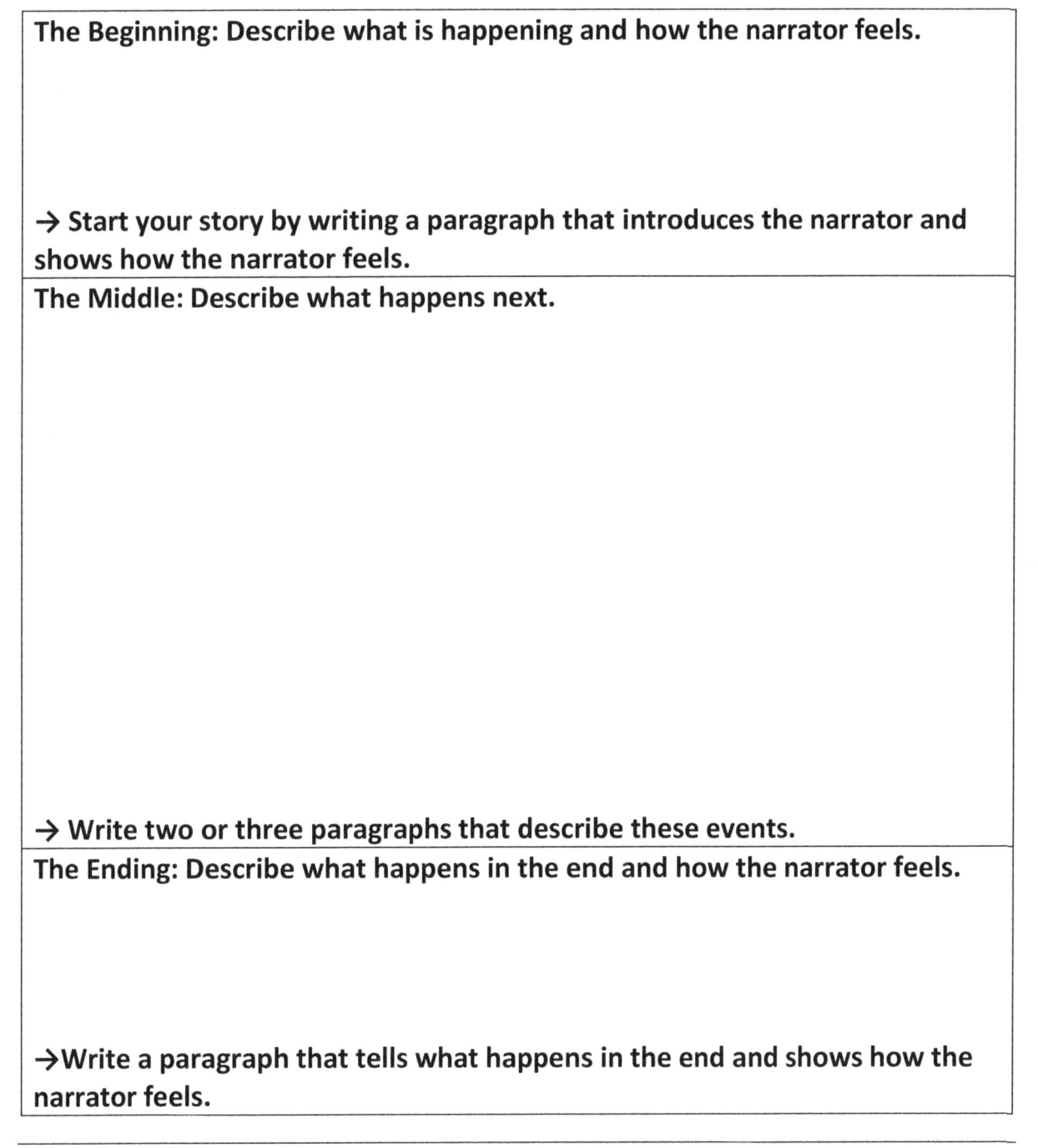

Use the table below to plan your story. Write or type a story of about 1 page.

The Beginning: Describe what is happening and how the narrator feels.   → **Start your story by writing a paragraph that introduces the narrator and shows how the narrator feels.**
The Middle: Describe what happens next.   → **Write two or three paragraphs that describe these events.**
The Ending: Describe what happens in the end and how the narrator feels.   →**Write a paragraph that tells what happens in the end and shows how the narrator feels.**

Writing Prompt 54

Write a story from the point of view of a boy who has just been dropped from his school's basketball team.

Use the table below to plan your story. Write or type a story of about 1 page.

The Beginning: Describe what is happening and how the narrator feels.   → **Start your story by writing a paragraph that introduces the narrator and shows how the narrator feels.**
The Middle: Describe what happens next.   → **Write two or three paragraphs that describe these events.**
The Ending: Describe what happens in the end and how the narrator feels.   →**Write a paragraph that tells what happens in the end and shows how the narrator feels.**

Writing Prompt 55

Write a story from the point of view of a magician about to perform for the first time.

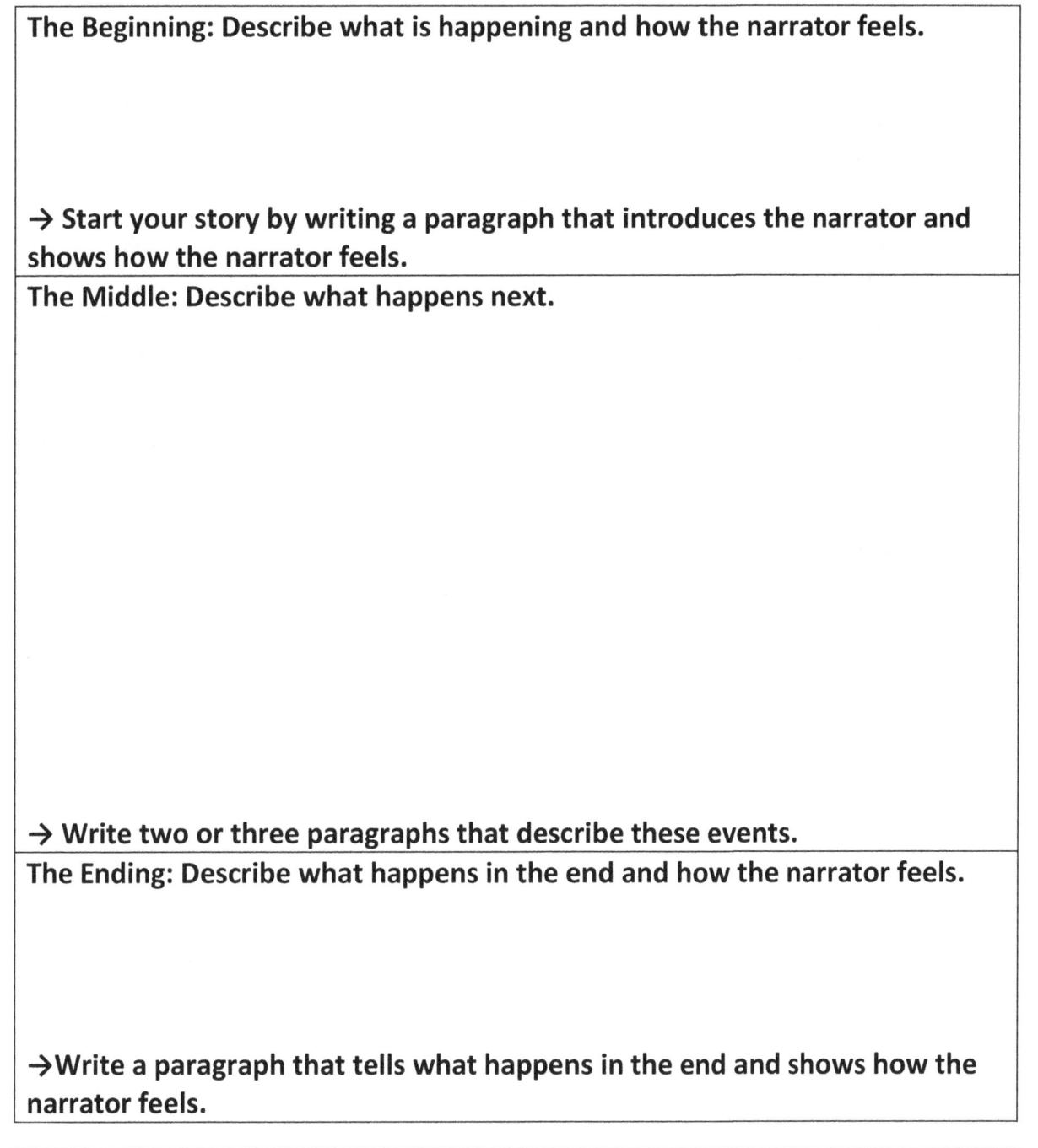

Use the table below to plan your story. Write or type a story of about 1 page.

The Beginning: Describe what is happening and how the narrator feels.   **→ Start your story by writing a paragraph that introduces the narrator and shows how the narrator feels.**
The Middle: Describe what happens next.   **→ Write two or three paragraphs that describe these events.**
The Ending: Describe what happens in the end and how the narrator feels.   **→Write a paragraph that tells what happens in the end and shows how the narrator feels.**

Warm-Up Exercise: Using Transition Words

In the next set, you will describe events in order. You will use words and phrases to tell when events occur, to show the order of events, or to show how much time has passed. The table below gives examples of words and phrases used for each purpose.

When Events Occur	Order of Events	How Much Time Passed
today	later	later that week
on Tuesday night	after	in less than an hour
in June	next	the day after
this week	afterwards	suddenly
at breakfast	first	at last
around noon	second	before I knew it
at midnight	before	after a long day
first thing this morning	last	many months later

Choose two examples of each type. Write a sentence that includes each word or phrase you chose.

When Events Occur

1. _____

2. _____

Order of Events

1. _____

2. _____

How Much Time Passed

1. _____

2. _____

Set 12: Understanding Sequence

Writing Prompt 56

Read the plot of a story about Cameron's last day of school.

> On the last day of school, Cameron cannot wait for his classes to end. He is looking forward to going on vacation.

The story will take place on the last day of school. It will begin at the start of the day and finish at the end of the school day. But it does not need to describe everything that happens for the whole day.

You can use transition words and phrases to move the story forward to the important parts of the day. These are words and phrases that tell when the events take place and to show how much time passed. For example, you might describe how lunchtime "dragged on slowly," or you might describe Cameron "finally going to the last class of the day." Use the plan below to complete the story. Write or type a story of about 1 page.

The Beginning: Describe what happens first.
Cameron arrives at school on the last day. He can hardly wait for the day to be over, so his vacation can start.
→ **Start your story by telling who the story is about and what is happening.**
The Middle: Describe what happens next.
The day drags on. Each class seems to take forever. Finally, there is just one class to go.
→ **Write two or three paragraphs that describe these events.**
The Ending: Describe what happens in the end.
The bell rings for the end of the last class. Cameron is excited that it is finally vacation time.
→ **End your story by writing a paragraph that describes these events.**

Writing Prompt 57

Write a story that begins with the sentence below.

As the sun went down, the forest quickly became completely dark.

Use the table below to plan your story. Write or type a story of about 1 page.

The Beginning: Describe what happens first.   → **Start your story by telling who the story is about and what is happening.**
The Middle: Describe what happens next.   → **Continue the story by telling what happens. You can use transition words and phrases to tell when events are happening.**
The Ending: Describe what happens in the end.   → **End your story by telling what happens. You can use transition words and phrases to tell when events are happening.**

Writing Prompt 58

Write a story that begins with the sentence below.

As the curtain rose, I saw the huge crowd for the first time.

Use the table below to plan your story. Write or type a story of about 1 page.

The Beginning: Describe what happens first.   → **Start your story by telling who the story is about and what is happening.**
The Middle: Describe what happens next.   → **Continue the story by telling what happens. You can use transition words and phrases to tell when events are happening.**
The Ending: Describe what happens in the end.   → **End your story by telling what happens. You can use transition words and phrases to tell when events are happening.**

Writing Prompt 59

Write a story that includes the sentence below. You can use the sentence at the start, middle, or end of your story.

Finally, this terrible day was almost over.

Use the table below to plan your story. Write or type a story of about 1 page.

The Beginning: Describe what happens first.   → **Start your story by telling who the story is about and what is happening.**
The Middle: Describe what happens next.   → **Continue the story by telling what happens. You can use transition words and phrases to tell when events are happening.**
The Ending: Describe what happens in the end.   → **End your story by telling what happens. You can use transition words and phrases to tell when events are happening.**

Narrative Writing Workbook, Grade 4

Writing Prompt 60

Write a story that includes the sentence below. You can use the sentence at the start, beginning, or end of your story.

At just past noon, I finally got the phone call I had been waiting for.

Use the table below to plan your story. Write or type a story of about 1 page.

The Beginning: Describe what happens first.   **→ Start your story by telling who the story is about and what is happening.**
The Middle: Describe what happens next.   **→ Continue the story by telling what happens. You can use transition words and phrases to tell when events are happening.**
The Ending: Describe what happens in the end.   **→ End your story by telling what happens. You can use transition words and phrases to tell when events are happening.**

Applying Writing Skills

The exercises in this section will provide practice writing different types of narrative texts. Each set focuses on one type of narrative writing.

Follow the instructions for each writing prompt, and plan your work in the space provided. Then write your work on a separate sheet of paper, or type your work.

After completing your work, review your writing. You can use the checklist on the next page to help you review your work.

Review Checklist

Organization
- ❏ Is there a beginning, a middle, and an ending?
- ❏ Is the beginning strong?
- ❏ Does the beginning introduce important details well?
- ❏ Is the middle well-organized?
- ❏ Do the events flow smoothly?
- ❏ Are words and phrases used to show event order?
- ❏ Is the ending strong?
- ❏ Does the ending tie up the story?

Content
- ❏ Are the actions of characters described well?
- ❏ Are descriptions used well?
- ❏ Are details used to describe things clearly?
- ❏ Are strong words used to help readers imagine the setting, the characters, or the events?

Grammar and Usage
- ❏ Are words spelled correctly?
- ❏ Is capitalization used correctly?
- ❏ Is punctuation used correctly?
- ❏ If dialogue is included, is it punctuated correctly?
- ❏ Are complete sentences used?
- ❏ Are sentences written correctly?
- ❏ Do the sentences make sense?
- ❏ Are words used correctly?

Narrative Writing Workbook, Grade 4

Set 13: Write from a Picture Prompt

Writing Prompt 61

Sometimes you will be asked to write a story based on a picture. Stories based on pictures should not just describe what the picture shows. Instead, you should think of an idea for a story based on the picture. Look at the picture below.

You can see that it shows a person fishing. You can use this person as the main character. Now think about a problem that the person could have. Base your story on how the character tries to solve the problem. One idea is that the person is stuck on a deserted island and has just worked out how to fish. Write down some other ideas you have below.

Notes and Ideas

Now choose the story idea you want to use. Use the table below to plan your story. Write or type a story of 1 to 2 pages.

The Beginning: Describe the main problem.
→ **Start your story by writing a paragraph that introduces the problem.**
The Middle: Describe how the character tries to solve the problem.
→ **Write two or three paragraphs that describe these events.**
The Ending: Describe how the problem is solved.
→**End your story by writing a paragraph that shows that the problem is solved.**

Writing Prompt 62

Look at the picture below. Write a story based on the picture.

You can use what is shown in the picture as the main problem of your story. Now think of a story idea based on what is shown. You can list some ideas or take notes below.

Notes and Ideas

Now choose the story idea you want to use. Use the table below to plan your story. Write or type a story of 1 to 2 pages.

The Beginning: Describe the main problem.   → **Start your story by writing a paragraph that introduces the problem.**
The Middle: Describe how the character tries to solve the problem.   → **Write two or three paragraphs that describe these events.**
The Ending: Describe how the problem is solved.   →**End your story by writing a paragraph that shows that the problem is solved.**

Writing Prompt 63

Look at the picture below. Write a story based on the picture.

You can use the person in the cart as the main character. You can make up all the other details about the person. The character could be in a serious race, could be driving a cart for the first time, or could be trying to overcome a fear. All these ideas would have a different problem. Choose an idea that you think would make a good story. You can list some ideas or take notes below.

Notes and Ideas

Now choose the story idea you want to use. Use the table below to plan your story. Write or type a story of 1 to 2 pages.

The Beginning: Describe the main problem.
→ **Start your story by writing a paragraph that introduces the problem.**
The Middle: Describe how the character tries to solve the problem.
→ **Write two or three paragraphs that describe these events.**
The Ending: Describe how the problem is solved.
→**End your story by writing a paragraph that shows that the problem is solved.**

Narrative Writing Workbook, Grade 4

Writing Prompt 64

Look at the picture below. Write a story based on the picture.

Use the picture to come up with a story idea based on a character's main problem. You can list some ideas or take notes below.

Notes and Ideas

Now choose the story idea you want to use. Use the table below to plan your story. Write or type a story of 1 to 2 pages.

The Beginning: Describe the main problem.   → **Start your story by writing a paragraph that introduces the problem.**
The Middle: Describe how the character tries to solve the problem.   → **Write two or three paragraphs that describe these events.**
The Ending: Describe how the problem is solved.   →**End your story by writing a paragraph that shows that the problem is solved.**

Set 14: Write a Personal Narrative

Writing Prompt 65

A personal narrative is a story that is based on events in your own life. Personal narratives usually tell about one event in your life. Just like a normal story, your personal narrative should have a beginning, a middle, and an ending. Think of it as writing a story where you are the main character. Your story should be written in first-person point of view.

When writing personal narratives, you will usually be given a topic to write about. Here is an example.

> Think of a time when something happened that surprised you. Write a story about a surprising event that happened to you.

To write this story, think of one surprising event from your life. Be sure to choose just one event to write about. Then plan a story based on this event. You can list some ideas or take notes below.

Notes and Ideas

Use the table below to plan your story. Write or type a story of 1 to 2 pages.

The Beginning: Introduce the important features of your story. You might tell where and when the events take place and what you are doing.   → **Start your story by writing a paragraph that sets the scene.**
The Middle: Describe the surprising event that happens.   → **Write two or three paragraphs that describe these events.**
The Ending: Describe what happens in the end. You might tell how the event ended or how you felt at this time.   → **Write a paragraph that concludes your story.**

Writing Prompt 66

Think of a time when you felt jealous of someone. What made you feel jealous? What did you do about how you felt?

Write a story about a time when you felt jealous of someone. You can list some ideas or take notes below.

> Remember that you do not have to state how you felt. Instead, you can use details and descriptions to show how you felt.

Notes and Ideas

Use the table below to plan your story. Write or type a story of 1 to 2 pages.

The Beginning: Introduce the important features of your story. You might tell where and when the events take place and what you are doing.
→ **Start your story by writing a paragraph that sets the scene.**
The Middle: Describe what made you feel jealous and what you did about it.
→ **Write two or three paragraphs that describe these events.**
The Ending: Describe what happens in the end. You might tell how the event ended or how you felt at this time.
→ **Write a paragraph that concludes your story.**

Writing Prompt 67

Think of a time when you had to stand up for yourself. Write a story about a time when you stood up for yourself. You can list some ideas or take notes below.

Think of this story as one based on a character solving a problem. In the beginning section, describe why you had to stand up for yourself. One story a student wrote was about his teammates not listening to him. The story started by introducing this problem. Describe your own main problem in the first section. In the middle section, describe how you solved the problem by standing up for yourself. In the last section, describe how the problem was solved or how you felt.

Notes and Ideas

Use the table below to plan your story. Write or type a story of 1 to 2 pages.

The Beginning: Describe the main problem.   → **Start your story by writing a paragraph that introduces the problem.**
The Middle: Describe how you solved the problem by standing up for yourself.   → **Write two or three paragraphs that describe these events.**
The Ending: Describe how the problem is solved or how you felt.   →**End your story by writing a paragraph that shows that the problem is solved.**

Writing Prompt 68

Think of a time when you helped someone. How did you help the person? How did it feel to help someone else?

Write a story about a time when you helped someone. You can list some ideas or take notes below.

Notes and Ideas

Use the table below to plan your story. Write or type a story of 1 to 2 pages.

The Beginning: Introduce the important features of your story. You might tell who you helped and why the person needed help.   → **Start your story by writing a paragraph that sets the scene.**
The Middle: Describe how you helped the person.   → **Write two or three paragraphs that describe these events.**
The Ending: Describe what happens in the end. You might tell how the event ended or how you felt at this time.   → **Write a paragraph that concludes your story.**

Set 15: Write an Animal Story

Writing Prompt 69

Animal stories use animals as characters, but the animals act more like people. The animals think, feel, and usually talk. Write a story based on the idea below.

An eagle is jealous of a parrot's bright colorful feathers.

Use the table below to plan your story. Write or type a story of 1 to 2 pages.

The Beginning: Describe who the character is and what the main problem is.   → **Start by writing a paragraph that introduces the character's problem.**
The Middle: Describe how the main character tries to solve the problem.   → **Write two or three paragraphs that describe these events.**
The Ending: Describe what happens in the end to solve the problem.   →**End your story by writing a paragraph that shows that the problem is solved.**

Writing Prompt 70

Write a story from the point of view of a dolphin. Think about what problem the dolphin could have.

Use the table below to plan your story. Write or type a story of 1 to 2 pages.

The Beginning: Describe who the character is and what the main problem is.   → **Start by writing a paragraph that introduces the character's problem.**
The Middle: Describe how the main character tries to solve the problem.   → **Write two or three paragraphs that describe these events.**
The Ending: Describe what happens in the end to solve the problem.   →**End your story by writing a paragraph that shows that the problem is solved.**

Writing Prompt 71

Write a story about two animals who cannot get along.

Use the table below to plan your story. Write or type a story of 1 to 2 pages.

The Beginning: Describe who the animals are and why they cannot get along.   → **Start by writing a paragraph that introduces the character's problem.**
The Middle: Describe what the two animals do to try to get along.   → **Write two or three paragraphs that describe these events.**
The Ending: Describe what happens in the end to solve the problem.   →**End your story by writing a paragraph that shows that the problem is solved.**

Writing Prompt 72

Write a story using the polar bear cub below as the main character.

Use the table below to plan your story. Write or type a story of 1 to 2 pages.

The Beginning: Describe who the character is and what the main problem is.   → Start by writing a paragraph that introduces the character's problem.
The Middle: Describe how the main character tries to solve the problem.   → Write two or three paragraphs that describe these events.
The Ending: Describe what happens in the end to solve the problem.   →End your story by writing a paragraph that shows that the problem is solved.

Set 16: Write an Adventure Story

Writing Prompt 73

Adventure stories usually have exciting events. The characters often face dangers. Many adventure stories are set in the wild. The characters might have to cross a dangerous river, climb a mountain, or escape from a pack of wolves.

Imagine that you are on a school trip. You are taking a tour through caves. Somehow, you get separated from the group. You are alone in the caves and you have to find your way out. Use the table below to plan an adventure story about your escape from the caves. Write or type a story of 1 to 2 pages.

The Beginning: Introduce the setting and the main character.   → Start your story by writing a paragraph that tells where the story is set and what is happening.
The Middle: Describe the exciting events that occur.   → Write two or three paragraphs that describe these events.
The Ending: Describe what happens in the end.   →End your story by writing a paragraph that describes these events.

Writing Prompt 74

Jackson looked down at the hill. It was steep and covered with white snow. He looked down at his skis. He hoped he was ready for this. Write a story about Jackson's downhill ski.

Use the table below to plan your story. Write or type a story of 1 to 2 pages.

The Beginning: Introduce the setting and the main character.   → **Start your story by writing a paragraph that tells where the story is set and what is happening.**
The Middle: Describe the exciting events that occur.   → **Write two or three paragraphs that describe these events.**
The Ending: Describe what happens in the end.   →**End your story by writing a paragraph that describes these events.**

Writing Prompt 75

Write a story about searching for a lost treasure.

Use the table below to plan your story. Write or type a story of 1 to 2 pages.

The Beginning: Introduce the setting and the main character.   **→ Start your story by writing a paragraph that tells where the story is set and what is happening.**
The Middle: Describe the exciting events that occur.   **→ Write two or three paragraphs that describe these events.**
The Ending: Describe what happens in the end.   **→End your story by writing a paragraph that describes these events.**

Writing Prompt 76

Look at the picture below. Write an adventure story based on the picture.

Use the table below to plan your story. Write or type a story of 1 to 2 pages.

The Beginning: Introduce the setting and the main character.   → Start your story by writing a paragraph that tells where the story is set and what is happening.
The Middle: Describe the exciting events that occur.   → Write two or three paragraphs that describe these events.
The Ending: Describe what happens in the end.   →End your story by writing a paragraph that describes these events.

Set 17: Write a Diary Entry

Writing Prompt 77

Sometimes you will be asked to tell a story in the form of a diary entry. A diary entry is written in first-person point of view and can be less formal than a story. A good diary entry is focused on telling about one event. A good way to write a diary entry is to start by stating what happened, to give details about what happened in the middle, and then to end with your thoughts on what happened.

Now imagine that you found out a secret today. Write a diary entry describing what the secret was and how you found out about it.

Use the table below to plan your writing. Write or type a diary entry of 1 to 2 pages.

The Beginning: Describe what the secret was and how you found out about it.   → Start your story by writing a paragraph that introduces the event.
The Middle: Describe what happened when you found out the secret.   → Write two or three paragraphs that describe these events.
The Ending: Describe how you feel about what happened.   → Write a paragraph that concludes your diary entry.

Writing Prompt 78

Imagine that you are a famous singer. Write a diary entry about an interesting event from your day.

Your diary entry will be in first-person point of view. You will write it as if you are the famous singer.

Use the table below to plan your writing. Write or type a diary entry of 1 to 2 pages.

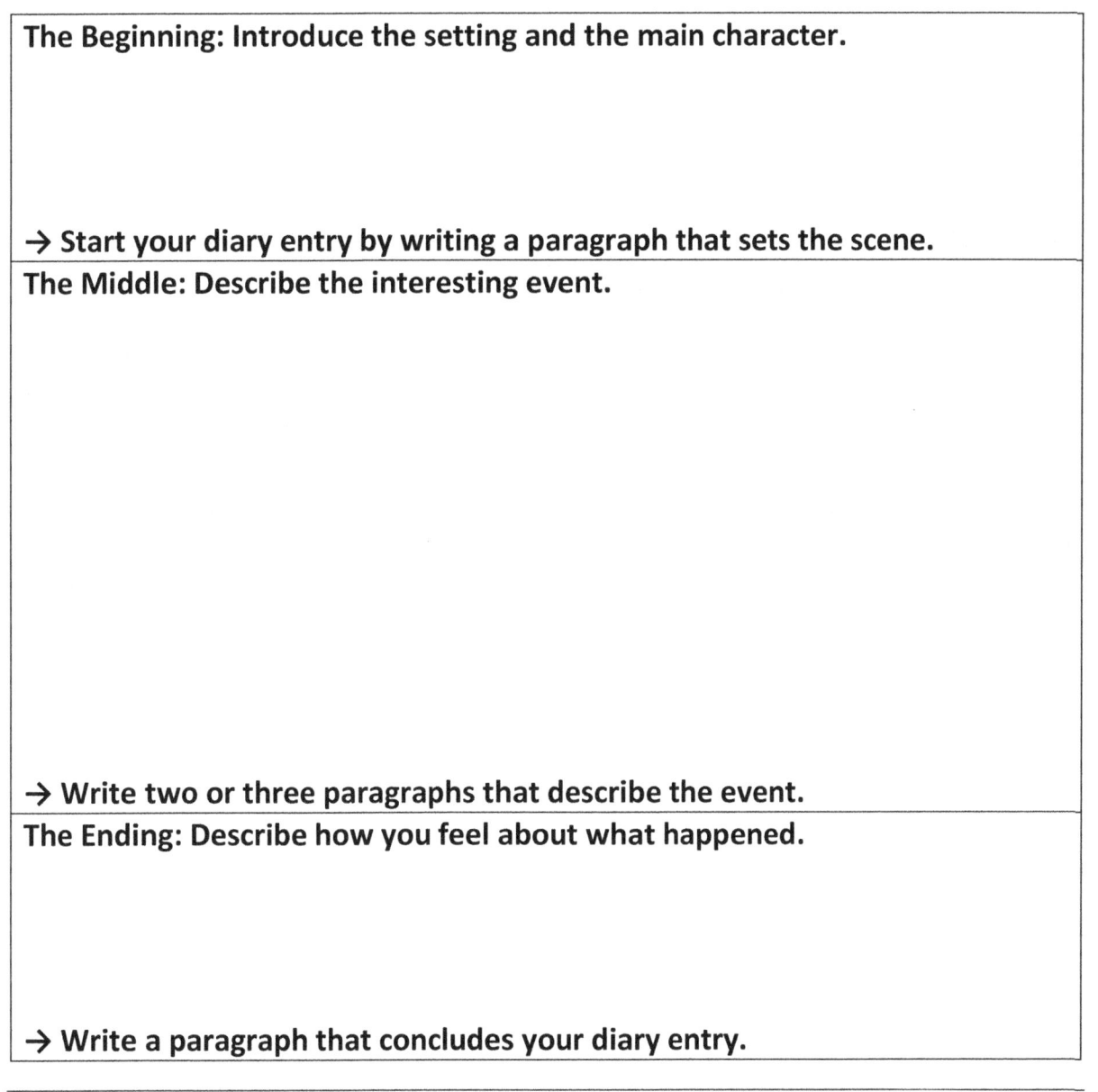

The Beginning: Introduce the setting and the main character.   → **Start your diary entry by writing a paragraph that sets the scene.**
The Middle: Describe the interesting event.   → **Write two or three paragraphs that describe the event.**
The Ending: Describe how you feel about what happened.   → **Write a paragraph that concludes your diary entry.**

Writing Prompt 79

Imagine that something very exciting happened to you today. Write a diary entry describing what happened.

> You do not need to write about something that actually happened. Make up an exciting event but describe it as if it really happened.

Use the table below to plan your writing. Write or type a diary entry of 1 to 2 pages.

The Beginning: Introduce the setting and the main character.
→ Start your diary entry by writing a paragraph that sets the scene.
The Middle: Describe the exciting event.
→ Write two or three paragraphs that describe the event.
The Ending: Describe how you feel about what happened.
→ Write a paragraph that concludes your diary entry.

Writing Prompt 80

Write a diary entry that starts with the sentences below.

Dear Diary,

I had been looking forward to Jerri's party for ages. I thought it would be a great party. But things really went wrong.

The prompt tells you that the diary entry should be about something that went wrong. You get to decide what went wrong.

Use the table below to plan your writing. Write or type a diary entry of 1 to 2 pages.

The Beginning: Introduce the party and tell what it is like at first.
→ Start your diary entry by writing a paragraph that sets the scene.
The Middle: Describe what went wrong at the party.
→ Write two or three paragraphs that describe these events.
The Ending: Describe how you feel about what happened.
→ Write a paragraph that concludes your diary entry.

Set 18: Write a Fantasy Story

Writing Prompt 81

A fantasy story is a story where the setting is not like real life. They often have characters like elves, dragons, wizards, monsters, fairies, and giants. Fantasy stories often involve some form of magic.

Think of an item that could have magic powers. Complete the title of the story by writing the item on the blank line. Then use the table below to plan your story. Write or type a story of 1 to 2 pages.

The Magic _____

The Beginning: Describe what the object is and what magic powers it has.   → **Start your story by writing a paragraph that introduces the object.**
The Middle: Describe a set of events where a character uses the magic object.   → **Write two or three paragraphs that describe these events.**
The Ending: Describe what happens in the end.   →**End your story by writing a paragraph that describes these events.**

Writing Prompt 82

Imagine that the object below comes to life. Write a story about what happens.

Use the table below to plan your story. Write or type a story of 1 to 2 pages.

The Beginning: Describe how the object comes to life.   → Start your story by writing a paragraph that tells how the object first comes to life.
The Middle: Describe what happens next.   → Continue the story by writing two or three paragraphs that show what happens when the object comes to life.
The Ending: Describe what happens in the end.   →End your story by writing a paragraph that describes these events.

Writing Prompt 83

Write a story that begins with the sentences below.

> "Please don't cast a spell on me," Jo cried. The witch giggled. She cast a spell anyway.

Use the table below to plan your story. Write or type a story of 1 to 2 pages.

The Beginning: Describe how a witch casts a spell on the character.   → **Start your story with a paragraph that tells how the witch casts the spell.**
The Middle: Describe what happens when the witch casts the spell.   → **Continue the story by writing two or three paragraphs that show what happens when the witch casts the spell.**
The Ending: Describe what happens in the end.   →**End your story by writing a paragraph that describes these events.**

Writing Prompt 84

Tori had a big problem. She decided it was time to call on her fairy godmother for help. The fairy godmother could cast a spell to make things better. Write a story about Tori's problem and how the fairy godmother solves it.

Use the table below to plan your story. Write or type a story of 1 to 2 pages.

The Beginning: Describe the main character and the main problem.   → **Start your story with a paragraph that introduces the character's problem.**
The Middle: Describe how the character tries to solve the problem.   → **Write two or three paragraphs that describe these events.**
The Ending: Describe how the problem is solved.   →**End your story by writing a paragraph that shows that the problem is solved.**

Set 19: Write a Science Fiction Story

Writing Prompt 85

Science fiction stories are made-up stories that involve science in some way. Science fiction stories sometimes involve time travel.

Imagine that you meet someone who claims they are visiting from the future. That person has an important message for you. Think of a story about what happens when you meet this person.

Use the table below to plan your story. Write or type a story of 1 to 2 pages.

The Beginning: Describe someone from the future giving you the message.   → **Start your story with a paragraph that tells what message you are given.**
The Middle: Describe what happens when you hear the message.   → **Continue the story by writing two or three paragraphs that describe what happens.**
The Ending: Describe what happens in the end.   → **End your story by writing a paragraph that concludes your story.**

Writing Prompt 86

Write a story that begins with the event described below.

> The computer suddenly turned itself on, opened a document, and began typing all by itself.

Use the table below to plan your story. Write or type a story of 1 to 2 pages.

The Beginning: Describe how the computer starts typing by itself.   → **Start your story with a paragraph that tells how the computer began typing.**
The Middle: Describe what happens next. You could describe what the computer types and what you do about it.   → **Continue the story by writing two or three paragraphs that describe what happens.**
The Ending: Describe what happens in the end.   → **End your story by writing a paragraph that concludes your story.**

Writing Prompt 87

Imagine that a pet store in the future allows you to design the perfect pet by combining any two animals. Write a story about the pet you design.

Use the table below to plan your story. Write or type a story of 1 to 2 pages.

The Beginning: Describe how you design a new pet and what two animals it combines.   → Start your story with a paragraph that introduces the pet.
The Middle: Describe what happens when you get the pet. You could describe something that goes wrong or how you have to get used to the strange pet.   → Continue the story by writing two or three paragraphs that describe what happens.
The Ending: Describe what happens in the end.   → End your story by writing a paragraph that concludes your story.

Writing Prompt 88

Write a story about the problem described below.

> A plant is designed that grows tomatoes in seconds. The tomatoes take over the yard and then the house.

Use the table below to plan your story. Write or type a story of 1 to 2 pages.

The Beginning: Describe the main problem.   → **Start your story by writing a paragraph that introduces the problem.**
The Middle: Describe how the main character tries to solve the problem.   → **Write two or three paragraphs that describe these events.**
The Ending: Describe how the problem is solved.   →**End your story by writing a paragraph that shows that the problem is solved.**

Set 20: Write a Mystery Story

Writing Prompt 89

A mystery story is a story where there is a mystery or a puzzle to be solved. Most mystery stories have three parts.

    The first part describes what the mystery is.
    The second part describes how a character tries to solve the mystery.
    The third part solves the mystery.

Use the table below to plan a mystery story about some strange footprints. You get to decide where the footprints are and what is strange about them. Write or type a story of 1 to 2 pages.

The Case of the Strange Footprints

The Beginning: Describe the mystery.   → **Start your story by writing a paragraph that introduces the mystery.**
The Middle: Describe how the main character tries to solve the mystery.   → **Write two or three paragraphs that describe these events.**
The Ending: Describe how the mystery is solved.   → **Write a paragraph that concludes your story.**

Writing Prompt 90

Write a mystery story with the title below.

The Haunted Clock

Mystery stories often have titles that describe the mystery. Use the title to come up with an idea for a story.

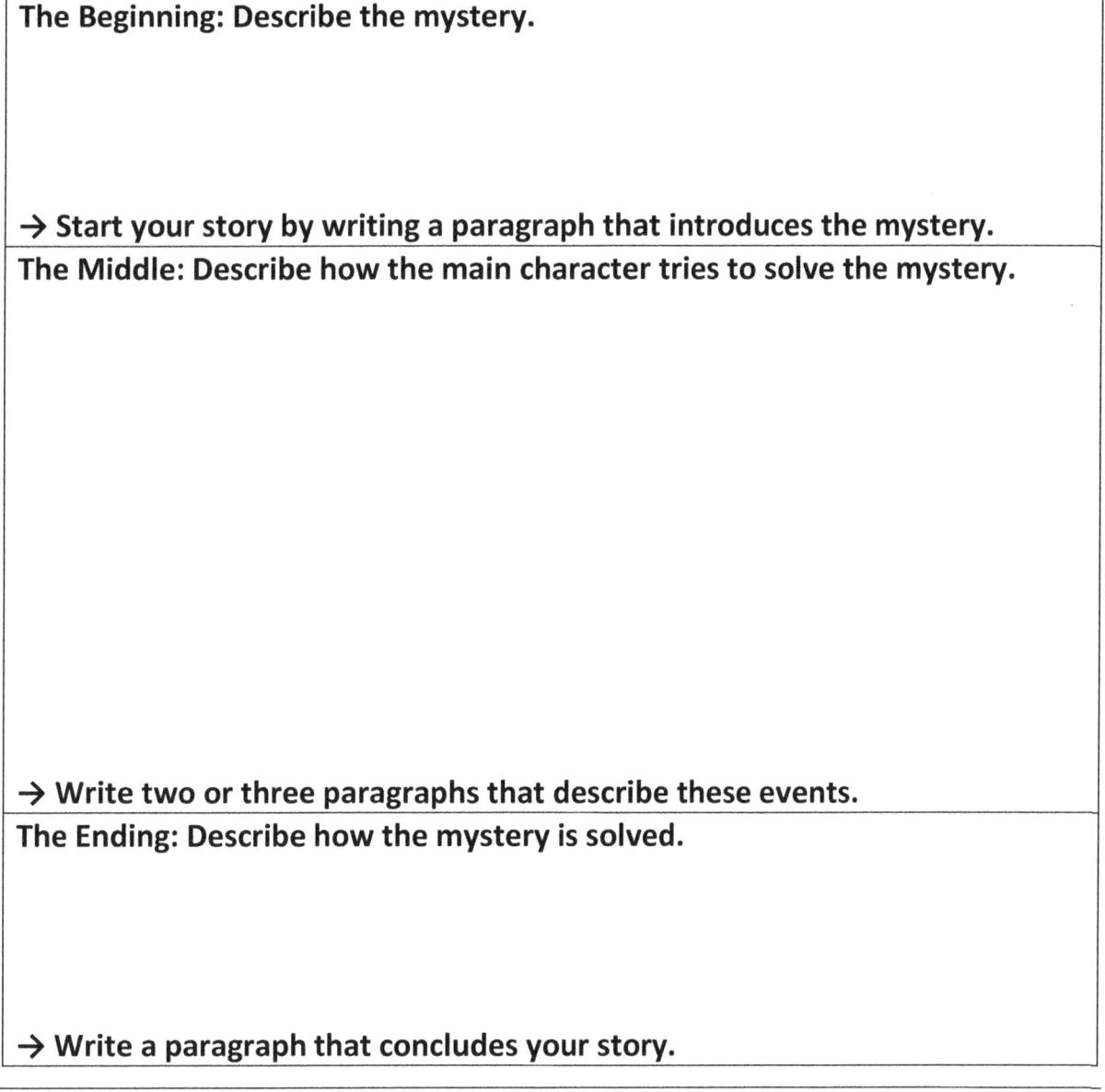

Use the table below to plan your story. Write or type a story of 1 to 2 pages.

The Beginning: Describe the mystery.   → Start your story by writing a paragraph that introduces the mystery.
The Middle: Describe how the main character tries to solve the mystery.   → Write two or three paragraphs that describe these events.
The Ending: Describe how the mystery is solved.   → Write a paragraph that concludes your story.

Writing Prompt 91

Write a mystery story with the title below.

The Chocolate Cupcakes Mystery

Use the table below to plan your story. Write or type a story of 1 to 2 pages.

The Beginning: Describe the mystery.   → **Start your story by writing a paragraph that introduces the mystery.**
The Middle: Describe how the main character tries to solve the mystery.   → **Write two or three paragraphs that describe these events.**
The Ending: Describe how the mystery is solved.   → **Write a paragraph that concludes your story.**

Writing Prompt 92

Write a mystery story with the title below.

A Voice in the Night

Use the table below to plan your story. Write or type a story of 1 to 2 pages.

The Beginning: Describe the mystery.   → **Start your story by writing a paragraph that introduces the mystery.**
The Middle: Describe how the main character tries to solve the mystery.   → **Write two or three paragraphs that describe these events.**
The Ending: Describe how the mystery is solved.   → **Write a paragraph that concludes your story.**

Set 21: Write a Real-Life Story

Writing Prompt 93

A real-life story is any story that describes events that could really happen. Real-life stories often describe problems that real people face. Use the problem described below to write a story.

Belinda forgets her lines during the school play.

Use the table below to plan your story. Write or type a story of 1 to 2 pages.

The Beginning: Describe the main problem.   → **Start your story by writing a paragraph that introduces the problem.**
The Middle: Describe how the main character tries to solve the problem.   → **Write two or three paragraphs that describe these events.**
The Ending: Describe what happens in the end to solve the problem.   →**End your story by writing a paragraph that shows that the problem is solved.**

Writing Prompt 94

When Tyra started at a new school, she wanted people to like her. She lied and told everyone her father was a famous actor. Now her new friends want to meet her famous father and she doesn't know what to do. Write a story about what happens next.

Use the table below to plan your story. Write or type a story of 1 to 2 pages.

The Beginning: Describe the main problem.   → **Start your story by writing a paragraph that introduces the problem.**
The Middle: Describe how the main character tries to solve the problem.   → **Write two or three paragraphs that describe these events.**
The Ending: Describe what happens in the end to solve the problem.   →**End your story by writing a paragraph that shows that the problem is solved.**

Writing Prompt 95

After Rachel won the race, she expected Jordana to be happy for her. Instead, Jordana would not even shake her hand. Rachel was proud of her win, but sad that her friend could not be happy for her. Write a story about what Rachel does to try to fix her friendship with Jordana.

> You could describe how Rachel tries to make things right or how she tries to talk to Jordana about how she feels.

Use the table below to plan your story. Write or type a story of 1 to 2 pages.

The Beginning: Describe the main problem.   → Start your story by writing a paragraph that introduces the problem.
The Middle: Describe how the main character tries to solve the problem.   → Write two or three paragraphs that describe these events.
The Ending: Describe what happens in the end to solve the problem.   →End your story by writing a paragraph that shows that the problem is solved.

Writing Prompt 96

Alex walked into the birthday party. As soon as he looked around, he remembered that it was a costume party. He was the only one who wasn't dressed up. He quickly walked back out. He needed to quickly come up with a costume idea. Write a story about how Alex makes a costume.

Use the table below to plan your story. Write or type a story of 1 to 2 pages.

The Beginning: Describe the main problem.   → **Start your story by writing a paragraph that introduces the problem.**
The Middle: Describe how the main character tries to solve the problem.   → **Write two or three paragraphs that describe these events.**
The Ending: Describe what happens in the end to solve the problem.   →**End your story by writing a paragraph that shows that the problem is solved.**

Set 22: Write a Letter

Writing Prompt 97

Some stories are told in the form of letters. Just like stories, the events are made up. However, you write them in first-person point of view as if you are writing to tell someone about the events. One good way to write a story in the form of a letter is described below.

The beginning introduces the topic or states what the letter is about.
The middle gives details about the topic or describes the events.
The ending sums up what happened or shows how the character feels.

Letters are less formal than many stories. You can write letters as if you are writing to a friend or family member to tell them something.

The table below shows a plan for a letter. Use the plan to write a letter. Write or type a letter of 1 to 2 pages.

The Beginning: Introduce the topic of the letter.
I stayed at my friend Helen's house, but we had a terrible time.
→ Start your letter by writing a paragraph that tells what the letter is about.
The Middle: Describe the main events.
We spent the whole time fighting. We couldn't agree on what movie to watch or what game to play. We fought over what pizza to get. I spent the whole time mad at her.
→ Write two or three paragraphs that describe these events.
The Ending: Summarize what happened or show how the character feels.
I am not sure if Helen and I can stay friends. I like her, but we have nothing in common. It makes me feel sad.
→End your letter by writing a paragraph that sums up the events.

Writing Prompt 98

Write a letter that describes how a character says something to someone that she wishes she could take back.

Use the table below to plan your letter. Write or type a letter of 1 to 2 pages.

The Beginning: Introduce the topic of the letter.   → Start your letter by writing a paragraph that tells what the letter is about.
The Middle: Describe the main events.   → Write two or three paragraphs that describe these events.
The Ending: Summarize what happened or show how the character feels.   →End your letter by writing a paragraph that sums up the events.

Writing Prompt 99

Write a letter that describes how a character wakes up feeling grumpy and later feels bad for ruining what could have been a good day.

Use the table below to plan your letter. Write or type a letter of 1 to 2 pages.

The Beginning: Introduce the topic of the letter.   → **Start your letter by writing a paragraph that tells what the letter is about.**
The Middle: Describe the main events.   → **Write two or three paragraphs that describe these events.**
The Ending: Summarize what happened or show how the character feels.   →**End your letter by writing a paragraph that sums up the events.**

Writing Prompt 100

Letters can also be about true events. You can write about events from your own life. Write a letter that describes something interesting that happened to you this week. The interesting event will be the topic of your letter.

Use the table below to plan your letter. Write or type a letter of 1 to 2 pages.

The Beginning: Introduce the topic of the letter.   → **Start your letter by writing a paragraph that tells what the letter is about.**
The Middle: Describe the main events.   → **Write two or three paragraphs that describe these events.**
The Ending: Summarize what happened or show how you feel.   →**End your letter by writing a paragraph that sums up the events.**

WRITING REVIEW AND SCORING GUIDE
For Parents, Teachers, and Tutors

Each set of writing prompts is designed to help students focus on one aspect of narrative writing or one genre of narrative writing. The scoring guides below list key factors that should be considered when reviewing writing tasks in each set.

After students have completed each writing task, review their work based on the factors listed. Identify strengths, weaknesses, and changes that can be made to improve their work. Give students guidance on what to focus on in the next writing task to improve their score.

Developing Writing Skills

Warm-Up Exercise: Relating Events to Each Other

The first three boxes should be completed with an event that would cause the last event. Any event can be accepted as long as it links the first and last event to show a complete plot. The last two boxes should be completed with an event that completes the plot.
Possible answers from top to bottom:
Dan gets halfway up and realizes he is scared of heights.
Lola uses up all her mother's baking goods.
Yuri wakes up in an empty bus at the bus depot.
The clown starts putting on a show in the shopping mall.
Kylie blames her brother for eating the meat patty.

Set 1: Understanding Plot

Review the student's work based on the following key factors.
- Is there a clear sequence of events?
- Does the story have a beginning, a middle, and an ending?
- Are the events described in order?
- Is the story focused on one set of events?
- Does the story have a clear ending?

Warm-Up Exercise: Problems and Solutions

The student should list four ways that each problem could be solved. Any solution can be accepted as long as it relates to the problem.

Note: Stories can describe events that could not really occur in real life. Students may need to be encouraged to use their imaginations to think of interesting or creative ways the problem could be solved.

Set 2: Using a Main Problem

Review the student's work based on the following key factors.
- Does the start of the story describe a main problem?
- Does the middle of the story describe how the problem is solved?
- Does the ending of the story include some sort of resolution?
- Are there clear transitions between events in the story?

Warm-Up Exercise: Using the Setting

The student should list four interesting events that could happen in each setting. Any answer can be accepted as long as it relates to the setting.

Set 3: Understanding Setting

Review the student's work based on the following key factors.
- Is the correct setting used?
- Is the story focused on a set of events taking place in the setting?
- Does the story have a beginning, a middle, and an ending?

Note: A common mistake made when writing based on setting is to focus too much on describing the setting. The setting should be thought of as the starting point for a story. It should be used to come up with an idea for events that occur in that setting.

Warm-Up Exercise: Characters Traits and Problems

The student should complete the table with a problem that each character could have because of the character trait described. Any answer can be accepted as long as the problem relates to the trait.

Set 4: Creating a Main Character

Review the student's work based on the following key factors.
- Is there one clear main character?
- Are the character's personality traits clearly shown?
- Does a series of events occur based on what the character is like?
- Does the end of the story include some sort of resolution?

Note: The resolution of the story can be that the character solves a problem, that the character changes, or that the character learns a lesson.

Warm-Up Exercise: Using Details to Show Feelings

The student should list actions that show how the character described feels. Any answer can be accepted as long as the actions relate to the feeling described. The student should finish by writing a complete paragraph that describes one of the characters given and how they feel. The paragraph can use the actions listed and any additional details.

Set 5: Using Descriptions

Review the student's work based on the following key factors.
- Does the student use descriptions to show what characters are like?
- Does the student use descriptions to show how characters feel?
- Are the descriptions effective at showing how characters feel?
- Does the story have a beginning, a middle, and an end?
- Does the character change during the story?

Set 6: Using Dialogue

Review the student's work based on the following key factors.
- Does the student include dialogue in the story?
- Is the dialogue effective at showing what is happening?
- Is the dialogue effective at showing how characters feel?
- Does the dialogue blend well with the rest of the story?
- Does the dialogue sound like how people really speak?

Note: Some students make the mistake of trying to write a whole story in dialogue. The key to using dialogue is to use it as a technique within a story.

Warm-Up Exercise: Characters Learning Lessons

The student should complete each diagram by describing what happens to teach the character the lesson described. Any answer can be accepted as long as it gives a reasonable series of events that would teach the lesson.
Possible answers from top to bottom:
Sue gets the cake out early. When she serves it, it oozes everywhere. / Sue wishes she had waited.
The new boy is fast and skilled. He is so good that Louis asks him for some tips. / Louis realizes that being tall is not all that matters.

Set 7: Understanding Theme

Review the student's work based on the following key factors.
- Does the story have a clear theme or a clear message?
- Are the events of the story based on a theme?
- Is there a main character who learns a lesson?
- Is there a clear sequence of events?
- Does the story have a beginning, a middle, and an ending?
- Can the reader understand the theme without it being stated?
- Is it clear that the main character has changed or has learned a lesson?

Set 8: Starting Strong

Review the student's work based on the following key factors.
- Does the story have a strong start?
- Does the opening paragraph introduce the character, the setting, and the problem?
- Does the middle of the story describe how the problem is solved?
- Does the ending of the story include some sort of resolution?
- Are there clear transitions between events in the story?

Warm-Up Exercise: Choosing Descriptive Words

The student should complete each question by replacing the underlined adjective with a stronger adjective. Strong answers will choose an adjective that tells more about what is being described. Possible answers are given below.
1. foul 2. freezing 3. blaring 4. teeny 5. massive

Warm-Up Exercise: Choosing Action Words

The student should complete each question by replacing the underlined verb with a stronger verb. Strong answers will choose a verb that relates to the event described in the sentence and suggests how something was done or how the person doing something feels. Possible answers are given below.
1. stormed   2. sped   3. gazed   4. hurled   5. clung

Set 9: Using Concrete Details

Review the student's work based on the following key factors.
- Does the student list concrete details for each scene?
- Do the concrete details help you imagine the scene?
- Are strong verbs and adjectives used?
- Are specific actions and details given?
- Does the student combine the details to effectively describe the scene?

Note: If the student lists vague details, you can improve each answer by encouraging the student to edit their work. You could point out verbs and adjectives that could be replaced with stronger words, or suggest that the student add an adjective.
For example, consider the following vague sentence and its edited version. The student was encouraged to add an adjective before the word *waves* and to replace the verb *big* with a stronger word.
The waves were big. → The rough waves were huge.

Set 10: Using Sensory Details

Review the student's work based on the following key factors.
- Does the student provide reasonable descriptions?
- Does each description focus on the sense given?
- Do the sensory details help you imagine the scene?
- Are strong verbs and adjectives used?
- Are specific details given?

Set 11: Using a Narrator

Review the student's work based on the following key factors.
- Is the story written in first-person point of view?
- Does the story show the narrator's feelings?
- Do the narrator's feelings change throughout the story?
- Does the narrator's voice suit the character?

Note: Voice refers to how the character sounds. A story with a young narrator will have a different voice than one with an older narrator. You may suggest that students think about how the character would sound if you were speaking to him or her. Then encourage students to write the story in the voice of the character.

Warm-Up Exercise: Using Transition Words

The student should write two sentences each using examples of words and phrases telling when events occur, the order of events, and how much time passed. Any sentence can be accepted as long as it uses the word or phrase in a reasonable way. Sample answers are given below.

When Events Occur
1. I heard the good news on Tuesday night.
2. At breakfast, I told Mom I was feeling sick.

Order of Events
1. After my sister left, I finally had a bedroom to myself.
2. First, we decided to draw a plan of the treehouse.

How Much Time Passed
1. We arrived in Miami before I knew it.
2. Many months later, I found a note hidden in my diary.

Set 12: Understanding Sequence

Review the student's work based on the following key factors.
- Is there a clear sequence of events?
- Does the story have a beginning, a middle, and an ending?
- Are transition words and phrases used to tell when events take place, and to transition between events?
- Are transition words and phrases used to show how much time has passed?
- Are the transition words and phrases used appropriate and effective?

Applying Writing Skills

Set 13: Write from a Picture Prompt

Review the student's work based on the following key factors.
- Is the story idea based on the picture?
- Is the story focused on one set of events?
- Does the story involve a character solving a problem?
- Does the story have a beginning, a middle, and an ending?
- Is the story well-organized with clear transitions?
- Are details and descriptions used effectively?
- Are strong and effective word choices used?
- Are there no or few errors in grammar and usage?

Note: Some students make the mistake of writing a description of what the picture shows. You may need to remind students to use the picture to come up with an idea for a story.

Set 14: Write a Personal Narrative

Review the student's work based on the following key factors.
- Is the story written in first-person point of view?
- Is the story focused on one set of events?
- Does the story have a beginning, a middle, and an ending?
- Is the story well-organized with clear transitions?
- Are the events clearly described?
- Is there some sort of resolution?
- Are details and descriptions used effectively?
- Are strong and effective word choices used?
- Are there no or few errors in grammar and usage?

Set 15: Write an Animal Story

Review the student's work based on the following key factors.
- Are the ideas well-developed?
- Are the characters well-developed?
- Does the story have a beginning, a middle, and an ending?
- Is the story well-organized with clear transitions?
- Is there some sort of resolution?
- Are details and descriptions used effectively?
- Are strong and effective word choices used?
- Are there no or few errors in grammar and usage?

Set 16: Write an Adventure Story

Review the student's work based on the following key factors.
- Is the setting established well?
- Does the story have a beginning, a middle, and an ending?
- Is the story well-organized with clear transitions?
- Is there some sort of resolution?
- Are details and descriptions used effectively?
- Are strong and effective word choices used?
- Are the events described in a way that makes them seem exciting?
- Are there no or few errors in grammar and usage?

Note: Adventure stories are a good opportunity for students to practice using descriptions. Descriptions can be used to help show how great the problems are, or to add a sense of excitement or suspense to the events. For example, descriptions could be used in the first story to show how dark and scary the caves are and to show how keen the character is to escape from the caves.

Set 17: Write a Diary Entry

Review the student's work based on the following key factors.
- Are the ideas well-developed?
- Is the diary entry focused?
- Is there a clear sequence of events?
- Does the diary entry have a beginning, a middle, and an ending?
- Does the diary entry include details and descriptions?
- Is there some sort of resolution?
- Are there no or few errors in grammar and usage?

Note: Diary entries are a good opportunity for students to develop a voice. Remind students that a diary entry does not have to be formal. They can write it in a casual way. They can also write it how they imagine the character would speak.

Set 18: Write a Fantasy Story

Review the student's work based on the following key factors.
- Are the ideas well-developed?
- Is there an element of fantasy or magic?
- Is there a clear sequence of events?
- Does the story have a beginning, a middle, and an end?
- Does the story include details and descriptions?
- Is there some sort of resolution?
- Are there no or few errors in grammar and usage?

Set 19: Write a Science Fiction Story

Review the student's work based on the following key factors.
- Is the story based on one well-developed idea?
- Does the story have a beginning, a middle, and an ending?
- Is the story well-organized with clear transitions?
- Is there some sort of resolution?
- Are details and descriptions used effectively?
- Are strong and effective word choices used?
- Are there no or few errors in grammar and usage?

Set 20: Write a Mystery Story

Review the student's work based on the following key factors.
- Is the story based on one well-developed idea?
- Does the story have a beginning, a middle, and an ending?
- Is the story well-organized with clear transitions?
- Is there a resolution where the mystery is solved?
- Are details and descriptions used effectively?
- Are strong and effective word choices used?
- Are there no or few errors in grammar and usage?

Set 21: Write a Real-Life Story

Review the student's work based on the following key factors.
- Is the character and the character's problem established well?
- Is the story well-organized with clear transitions?
- Is the story focused on a character solving a problem?
- Is there some sort of resolution?
- Are details and descriptions used effectively?
- Are strong and effective word choices used?
- Are there no or few errors in grammar and usage?

Set 22: Write a Letter

Review the student's work based on the following key factors.
- Is the letter written in first-person point of view?
- Is the letter focused on one set of events?
- Does the letter have a beginning, a middle, and an ending?
- Is the letter well-organized with clear transitions?
- Are the events clearly described?
- Does the letter show how the narrator feels?
- Does the letter end with an effective summary or resolution?
- Are details and descriptions used effectively?
- Are strong and effective word choices used?
- Are there no or few errors in grammar and usage?

Made in the USA
Middletown, DE
18 March 2020